UNITED NATIONS

WORLD YOUTH REPORT

YOUTH EMPLOYMENT:

YOUTH PERSPECTIVES ON THE PURSUIT OF DECENT WORK IN CHANGING TIMES

UNWorldYouthReport.org

1

World Youth Report

Published by the United Nations

New York, New York 10017, United States of America

ST/ESA/338

United Nations Publication

Copyright © United Nations, 2013

All rights reserved

All queries or rights and licenses including subsidiary rights should be addressed to United Nations Publications, 300 East 42nd

Street, New York, NY 10017, United States of America; email: publications@un.org; website: un.org/publications.

ISBN = 978-92-1-130319-3

eISBN = 978-92-1-055866-2

United Nations Publication Sales no. E.12.IV.6

Note: The designations employed and the presentation of the material in this publication do not imply the expression of any opinion whatsoever on the part of the Secretariat of the United Nations concerning the legal status of any country or territory or of its authorities, or concerning the delimitations of its frontiers. The term "country" as used in the text of the present report also refers, as appropriate, to territories or areas. The designations of country groups in the text and the tables are intended solely for statistical or analytical convenience and do not necessarily express a judgment about the stage reached by a particular country or area in the development process. Mention of the names of firms and commercial products does not imply the endorsement of the United Nations.

Technical Notes: In this publication, unless otherwise indicated, the term "youth" refers to all those between the ages of 15 and 24, as reflected in the World Programme of Action for Youth. The term "young people" may be used interchangeably with the word "youth." The United Nations Secretariat cannot independently verify all details contained in the comments posted to its 11 October–7 November 2011 e-discussion on youth employment (available from bit.ly/obK7Qm) which are reproduced, directly or indirectly, herein. Comments posted to the e-discussion on youth employment which are directly quoted in the present publication may have been altered by the United Nations Secretariat for clarity and grammatical purposes.

Front Cover Photo: Girl scouts and boy scouts participating in the "Eyes of Darfur" project hold up their cameras at El Fasher's Youth Committee Center in North Darfur, Sudan, 10 April 2011, El Fasher, Sudan. UN Photo / Albert Gonzalez Farran

Graphic Design: Graphic Design Unit, Outreach Division, Department of Public Information, United Nations, New York

UNWorldYouthReport.org

The World Youth Report is also available online at unworldyouthreport.org with added digital features.

THE DEPARTMENT OF ECONOMIC AND SOCIAL AFFAIRS

of the United Nations Secretariat is a vital interface between global policies in the economic, social and environmental spheres and national action. The Department works in three main interlinked areas: (i) it compiles, generates and analyses a wide range of economic, social and environmental data and information on which Member States of the United Nations draw to review common problems and to take stock of policy options; (ii) it facilitates the negotiations of Member States in many intergovernmental bodies on joint courses of action to address ongoing or emerging global challenges; and (iii) it advises interested governments on the ways and means of translating policy frameworks developed in United Nations conferences and summits into programmes at the country level and, through technical assistance, helps build national capacities.

Haitians Plant and Save Land in Cash-for-Work Program
UN Photo/Logan Abassi | May 2012 | Port-au-Prince

ACKNOWLEDGEMENTS

The United Nations Department of Economic and Social Affairs is grateful for the many contributions received to the 11 October-7 November 2011 e-discussion on youth employment from young people and representatives of youth-led organizations around the world, who enabled each other as well as viewers of the e-discussion to learn from their views and experiences. The Department wishes to convey special thanks to Ms. Sarah Huxley, who ably led the moderation of the e-discussion, prepared material for the present report, and provided significant overall support to the development of the World Youth Report 2011. The Department also appreciates the efforts of the following distinguished weekly moderators of the e-discussion: Mr. Sergio Andrés Iriarte Quezada, International Labour Organization (Week 1); Ms. Maria Cavatore, Plan International (Week 2); Professor Julian D. May, Ms. Kathleen Diga and the team at the University of KwaZulu-Natal, the United Nations Academic Impact hub on poverty (Week 3); and Mr. Luis David Sena, Youth Delegate of the Dominican Republic to the United Nations (Week 4).

The Department of Economic and Social Affairs is pleased to thank several resource volunteers who provided valuable support throughout the e-discussion: Mr. Nikola Panduric; Mr. Saji Prelis; Ms. Kirthi Jayakumar; Mr. Marcelo Renjel; Ms. Steffi Jochim; Mr. Amadou Moctar Diallo; Ms. Lara Kaplan; Ms. Hira Hafeez; and Mr. Eddie Ombagi. The Department would like to further recognize the following participants for their commitment in contributing to the e-discussion: Seabe, age 23, from Botswana; Yasmyn, age 24, from Guadeloupe; Loubna, age 23, from Morocco; and Ayshah, age 26, from Kenya. The Department is additionally grateful to the following participants for sharing their case studies: Yasmyn, age 24, from Guadeloupe; Emad, age 28, from Egypt; Hira, age 23, from Pakistan; Enass, age 25, from Jordan; and Loubna, age 23, from Morocco.

The United Nations Department of Economic and Social Affairs appreciates the support provided by the United Nations Academic Impact to the e-discussion on youth employment. The Department also extends special thanks to Ms. Monique Coleman, United Nations Youth Champion, and Mr. Ronan Farrow, Special Advisor on Global Youth Issues to the United States Secretary of State, for engaging with young people on youth employment issues via Twitter as special features of the e-discussion.

The United Nations Department of Economic and Social Affairs wishes to thank the following for their photo contributions: Mr. Adrian Fisk, of the iSpeak Global project, and 7 Billion Actions, a global movement for all humanity led by the United Nations Population Fund; Ms. Mia Collis; the International Labour Organization; the United Nations Development Programme; the United Nations Educational, Scientific and Cultural Organization; and several young participants in the e-discussion, including Lara, Maria, Michael, Nikola, Shahbaz, Ayshah, Nady, Abhimanyu, Amadou, Carolina, Efehi, Kirthi, and Nduta.

A group of youth practice capoeira on the beach
preparation for International Youth D
UN Photo/Martine Perret | July 2010 | Dili, Timor-Le

CONTENTS

5 ACKNOWLEDGEMENTS

9 INTRODUCTION

15 EMPLOYMENT & YOUTH: THE SITUATION OF YOUNG PEOPLE IN THE LABOUR MARKET AND KEY TRENDS

39 PREPARING FOR WORK

63 LOOKING FOR A JOB

83 YOUTH AT WORK

101 CONCLUSIONS & RECOMMENDATIONS

109 REFERENCES

Young people themselves are crucial stakeholders in the pursuit of decent and productive work for all. They are **rights-holders** and **active participants** in society, in addition to representing the future global workforce; often times, they are also **pioneers.**

UN Photo/Patricia Esteve
November 2011 | DAgboville, Côte d'Ivoire

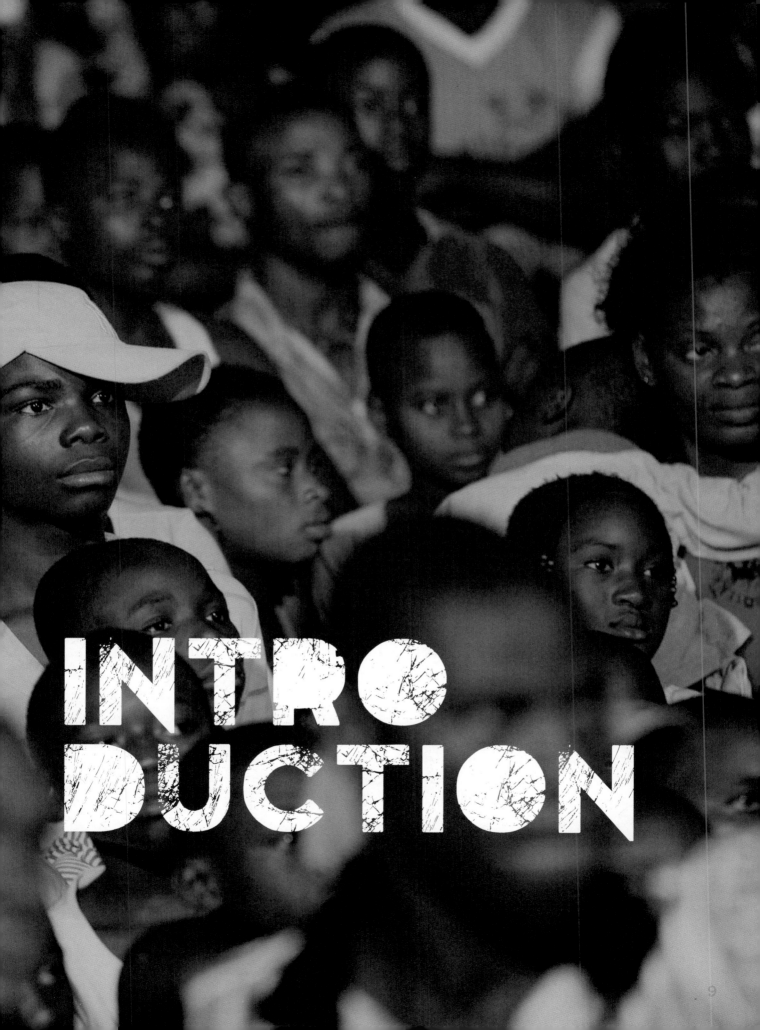

INTRODUCTION

HOW THIS REPORT WAS PRODUCED

The present report[1] is largely based on an e-discussion with young people and representatives of youth-led organizations on the transition from schools and training institutions into the world of work. The online consultation, intended to contribute directly to this report, took place from 11 October to 7 November 2011 using the IntenseDebate commenting platform on the website of the United Nations Department of Economic and Social Affairs (UNDESA). Participants were requested to share their own views, experiences and recommendations on preparing for, entering, and remaining active in the labour force. Throughout each week, one broad theme was explored – corresponding to a chapter of the present report – from a social lens and through diverse perspectives. UNDESA invited the participation of young people aged 15 to 30 – taking into account both the United Nations Secretariat's definition of youth and many local cultural contexts and understandings – as well as representatives of youth-led organizations, although the e-discussion was accessible to all. The e-discussion was conducted mainly in the English language, but participants were also invited to post comments in the French and Spanish languages. Many posts were translated on a volunteer basis, and Google Translate was also made available on the platform.

The United Nations Department of Economic and Social Affairs (UNDESA) additionally welcomed contributions in the form of postings, votes and uploads of photos, videos and other resources related to the theme of youth employment onto the United Nations International Year of Youth Facebook page as well as messages (tweets) to the Twitter account of the United Nations Focal Point on Youth.

The United Nations Department of Economic and Social Affairs (UNDESA) engaged a consultant, Ms. Sarah Huxley, to manage and serve as lead moderator of the e-discussion as well as to prepare several chapters of the present report. Throughout the e-discussion, UNDESA and Ms. Huxley were also generously supported by volunteer weekly moderators as well as several volunteer resource persons.

The e-discussion was actively promoted by the United Nations Department of Economic and Social Affairs (UNDESA) and other members of the United Nations Inter-agency Network on Youth Development, UN Academic Impact, and other partners and volunteers, including among civil society networks and through social media channels.

As the World Youth Report 2011 is based mainly on contributions to the e-discussion, it must be acknowledged that the report may not accurately reflect the average views of young people or the range of diversity among youth. Extensive outreach efforts were made to reach as many young people as possible, paying due attention to geographic, age, gender and other considerations, with information on participation in the e-discussion. Additionally, the "ways of working" contained

[1] The World Youth Report is a biennially recurring publication of the United Nations (see resolution E/2007/26).

on the e-discussion platform reminded participants to value and respect one another's thoughts and opinions, and requested that, where possible, participants assist young people without access to a computer or internet services to also participate in the e-discussion.

THE CONTEXT: A GROWING SPOTLIGHT ON GLOBAL YOUTH ISSUES

The transition of young people into work marks a critical period in the life cycle. It signifies a crucial stage of independence, the application of academic learning, and social and economic productivity, as well as sets the stage for an individual's potential in terms of earning capacity, job options and the possibility of advancement. In effect, the manner in which a young person enters the work force influences his or her life-long employment experiences. When and how this transition occurs further impacts the well-being of that person as well as his/her relationships with family, friends, community and society.

With less experience and fewer skills than many adults, young people often encounter particular difficulty accessing work. The global youth unemployment rate, which has long exceeded that of other age groups, saw its largest annual increase on record in 2009; at its peak, 75.8 million young people were unemployed.[2] Even after finding work, young workers continue to confront job instability, few opportunities for skills development and advancement, and joblessness. They are more likely to be in vulnerable jobs, which can further adversely affect their future livelihood and income prospects. In fact, young people make up a disproportionate number of the world's working poor. Data on the working poor, many of whom work in the informal economy, is limited. However, where data is available, "youth accounted for 23.5 per cent of the total working poor, compared with only 18.6 per cent of non-poor workers".[3]

The employment scenario for young people has been worsened by the lingering global economic crisis, and the current situation of youth employment poses an urgent challenge with long-term implications for both young people and society. At the same time, not since 1995 – when Member States of the United Nations adopted the World Programme of Action for Youth to the Year 2000 and Beyond – has there been such a spotlight directing the international community's attention to global youth issues. Young people's employment concerns were one of the central issues highlighted during the International Year of Youth (August 2010-August 2011), which culminated in a High- Level Meeting of the General Assembly on Youth in July 2011. The outcome document of the High-Level Meeting clearly identifies youth employment as a critical challenge that requires an urgent response by governments as well as the international community.

[2] International Labour Organization, 2011b, pp. 1-2.
[3] ibid., p. 5

In some cases, the challenge of youth employment is driven by fears of civil unrest. There is no doubt that one of the contributing factors to the recent Arab Spring uprisings is the disturbingly high levels of youth unemployment in the Middle East and North Africa region. The total youth unemployment rate in 2010 was 25.5 per cent in the Middle East and 23.8 per cent in North Africa. Female youth unemployment in these regions was particularly striking, at 39.4 per cent in the Middle East and 34.1 per cent in North Africa.[4] Yet, for most stakeholders, the focus on youth employment is fundamentally shaped by such questions as: How do we and our societies create, enable and champion young people's participation in local and global economies in a meaningful and dynamic way? How do we foster, nurture and let flourish the capabilities of each young person in our society?

This online interactive report aims to shed light on some of these complex questions. Yet it also enables young people from around the globe to share, challenge, discuss and debate: What are young people themselves doing to address these challenges? Where and how are young people succeeding in employment? What more can governments do to help young people prepare for the transition from education to work? How can youth themselves become more active in decision-making processes, such as developing relevant curricula?

[4] ibid., p. 10

OVERVIEW OF THE REPORT

Chapter I introduces the status of young people in the labour market and youth employment trends. It provides a snapshot of key youth employment-related demographics, highlighting the critical role of youth employment in social development. The chapter also considers positive and negative trends across countries in various stages of development to illustrate the state of youth employment world-wide.

Chapter II explores education, as the foundation for working life, with focus on views regarding educational quality and utility. Vocational education, life skills and entrepreneurship are highlighted. The chapter examines what some schools are doing, and what more can be done, to help young people transition to work. It considers ways for educational systems to be more responsive to the changing needs of economies and societies, and labour markets in particular. It also looks at ways in which young people may hold policymakers and decision-makers accountable for fulfilling the right to quality education.

Chapter III focuses on the transition of young people into work, particularly the search for a first job. It examines the availability among youth of information on labour markets and job seeking, and explores various mechanisms and tools to inform and advise young people, from networking to subsidized employment programmes. The chapter also looks into potential emerging areas of opportunity for young people.

Chapter IV explores the quality and conditions of jobs held by youth, and how young people's working situation interacts with their family and home lives. It addresses high rates among youth of underemployment, participation in the informal economy, vulnerable employment, wages and working conditions. The chapter also examines how a lack of decent work opportunities can influence family life, social processes such as marriage and fertility, as well as health and well-being.

Young people themselves are crucial stakeholders in the pursuit of decent and productive work for all. They are rights-holders and active participants in society, in addition to representing the future global workforce; often times, they are also pioneers. Yet, too frequently, their voices go unheard and their positive and negative experiences and viewpoints unshared, particularly with decision-makers. The present report takes heed of calls by Member States, youth-led and youth-focused organizations, young people and others to bring young people's voices into fora where youth issues are discussed and acted upon. Therefore, the World Youth Report 2011 is intended above all to explore youth employment issues mainly through the words of young people themselves around the world.

"How are we supposed to gain experience if we are not even presented with an opportunity to start working?"
– Mridula, 16

UN Photo/Staton Winter
May 2010 | Tubmanburg, Liberia

CHAPTER I
EMPLOYMENT & YOUTH

The Situation of Young People in the Labour Market and Key Trends

GROWING GAPS IN DECENT WORK FOR YOUNG PEOPLE IN THE AFTERMATH OF THE GLOBAL ECONOMIC CRISIS

Across regions, young people are disproportionately affected by unemployment, underemployment, vulnerable employment and working poverty. Even during periods of economic growth, many economies have been unable to absorb large youth populations into the labour market. In recent years, however, the global financial and economic crisis has further hit young people particularly hard in the developed world.

THE CONTEXT: A GROWING SPOTLIGHT ON GLOBAL YOUTH ISSUES

World-wide, rates of young people's participation in the labour force have been in decline. Between 1998 and 2008, the youth labour force participation rate fell from 54.7 to 50.8 per cent.[1] In 2009, against a total global unemployment rate of 6.3 per cent[2], the global youth unemployment rate peaked at 12.7 per cent, representing 75.8 million unemployed youth, marking the largest annual increase over the 20 years of available global estimates.[3] Youth unemployment rates are significantly higher than adult rates in all geographic regions, though with considerable variation. In 2010, the global youth unemployment rate remained at 12.6 per cent (despite a marginal reduction in the absolute number of job- seeking youth), dramatically overshadowing the global adult unemployment rate of 4.8 per cent.[4] Declines in youth labour force participation rates may indicate that young people are instead engaged in full-time schooling or training. However, in parallel with recent high unemployment rates, they more likely suggest that many young people have stopped looking for work, and that, were they to continue to seek work, actual unemployment rates would rise even further.

[1] International Labour Organization, 2010, p. 3
[2] International Labour Organization, 2011a, p. 12
[3] International Labour Organization, 2011b, p. 4
[4] International Labour Organization, 2011a and United Nations, Department of Economic and Social Affairs, Population Division, 2011

"Decent work" defined

According to the International Labour Organization, "decent work" refers to the overall aspirations of people in their working lives. It consists of four pillars: job creation, rights at work, social protection and social dialogue, with gender equality as a cross-cutting objective.

There are several reasons for this. During economic downturns, young people are often the "last in" and the "first out" – the last to be hired, and the first to be dismissed. Young workers have less work experience than older workers, which is highly valued by employers. This issue has particularly severe implications for the school to work transition, the period when young people enter the labour market to look for their first job. Employment is often associated with young people's entry into adulthood and independence, and is of course vital as a source of income for individuals and families.

Young people often face extended periods of joblessness and many become discouraged. They may stop seeking employment opportunities and decide to drop out of the labour market altogether (at which point they are no longer defined as officially unemployed). Many choose to "hide out" in educational institutions, and others engage in volunteer work. They seek to build knowledge, experience or new skills while they wait for better job opportunities. Some may accept multiple part-time jobs in order to try to piece together an adequate income. Several countries have seen recent increases both in part-time youth employment as well as time-related youth underemployment, which indicates that an individual would like to have more working hours than s/he currently does.[5] In some cases, youth are simply inactive – neither at work or in school. Young people who live in extreme poverty, however, cannot afford to be inactive, go back to school or "hide out". They simply have to find some way of making a living, often accepting low-paid and poor quality jobs, especially in the informal economy. The challenge is to bring them to the formal sector or to rewarding self-employment.

[5] International Labour Organization, 2011b, p. 4

THE SITUATION OF YOUTH EMPLOYMENT: TRENDS AND YOUNG PEOPLE'S VIEWS

From 11 to 17 October (Week I) 2011, the United Nations e-discussion on youth employment was open to all to share views and discuss the overall situation of young people in the labour market as well as key trends in youth employment. There were more than 300 comments posted by young people world-wide. Participation was particularly high from the African region. The e-discussion, which solicited the views of young people aged 15 to 30[6] as well as those of representatives of youth-led organizations, received comments during week I from young men and women between the ages of 16 and 30. In addition, more than 700 people accessed and viewed the platform during the week.

This chapter provides an overview of the global situation of young people in the labour market together with comments from young people stemming from actual experience and observations. It presents data and analysis of current youth employment-related research and aims to identify and briefly explore youth employment trends and issues across regions with different levels of development. In addition, the chapter provides highlights of views of young people from around the world. In large part, young people's contributions to the e-discussion align with and corroborate the prevailing research that describes significant challenges to decent work for young people. More importantly, however, their contributions illustrate these challenges on a personal level and capture how they are experienced from the perspective of youth themselves. As will become evident as the chapter progresses, young people have a lot to say on the matter of youth employment which reveals remarkable and valuable insight.

---

[6] This is taking into account both the United Nations definition of youth (15- to 24-year-olds) and many local cultural contexts and understandings.

YOUTH UNEMPLOYMENT, UNDEREMPLOYMENT AND VULNERABLE EMPLOYMENT

WHAT THE RESEARCH SHOWS

The need to provide more and better jobs for young people exists across countries. However, youth employment challenges tend to differ in developed and developing economies. The developed world has been most significantly affected by youth unemployment spikes due to the global economic crisis, and its core challenge is the provision of work opportunities for young people who are entering the labour market. Yet the developing countries are home to 87 per cent of the world's youth, who are often underemployed and working in the informal economy under poor conditions. The core challenge for these countries is to not only generate new employment opportunities for young people, but to also improve the quality of all jobs available to them.

In the Middle East and North Africa, a region which has made progress in educational levels among girls and boys, approximately 25 per cent of young people of working age are unemployed.[7] It is important to note that in low-income economies, young people have limited or no social safety nets on which to fall back, so that few young people can afford to stay out of work. For this reason, the unemployment rate does not capture the full extent of difficulties facing young people in developing economies, where youth are more likely to accept any job.

Youth unemployment has continued to worsen in the developed economies, where rates were higher in 2009 than at any time since measurement began in 1991.[8] Several countries of the European Union saw record-high rates of youth employment in 2011: 48.9 per cent in Spain and 45.1 per cent Greece.[9] In November 2011, the number of unemployed youth in the United Kingdom reached a record high of 1 million. In some of these countries, long-term unemployment rates are far higher among youth than adults. Moreover, in the countries of the Organization for Economic Cooperation and Development (OECD), 12.6 per cent of the youth population – representing 22.3 million young people – were inactive in the fourth quarter of 2010, neither in jobs nor in education or training, leaving them increasingly vulnerable to exclusion from the labour market.[10]

[7] ibid., p. 10
[8] ibid., p. 2
[9] European Commission, 2011
[10] Organization for Economic Cooperation and Development, 2011

A delayed transition from school to work – which may involve a period of unemployment or extended time in school – can have long-term adverse effects. Such a delay leads to erosion of skills, which may result cumulatively in lower life-time earnings. The longer youth remain disconnected, the more difficult it is to support their integration into the labour market. Yet, although temporary and part-time work can help young workers to enter the labour market, they also risk leading to persistent job insecurity. Similarly, a lack of decent work opportunities means that many young people, particularly in developing countries, end up working in low-paid and unsafe jobs which provide no prospects for development.

Young people in all regions are more likely than adults to be unemployed or to work in vulnerable employment. They are at greater risk of earning lower wages in a low-productivity job, working in unsafe or risky conditions, working below their skill or educational level, working long hours or fewer hours than needed, holding a temporary job, having few or no prospects for advancement and/or lacking job stability. Such disadvantages among youth in the work force also mean that many young workers lack bargaining power and are poorly positioned to organize towards improving their situation. Young women are particularly likely to be underemployed and in vulnerable jobs.[11]

Despite important gains in education among young women, their employment outcomes continue to lag behind those of young men. Globally, in 2010, 56.3 per cent of young males participated in the labour force, against 40.8 per cent of young females.[12] Where young women do participate in the labour market, they generally confront greater challenges in accessing jobs than do young men, i.e. they face higher unemployment compared to their male counterparts. When employed, they are also more likely to be in traditionally female occupations and unstable, part-time and lower-paid jobs. In several parts of the world, there remain significant gaps between young men's and young women's earnings. For instance, the hourly earnings of young women aged 15 to 24 are only 82 per cent and 84 per cent of men's in sub-Saharan Africa and East Asia and the Pacific, respectively. In some regions, however, young women are closing the wage gap with men faster than are older women due to their expanded access to educational opportunities over the last several years.[13] The recent economic crisis reduced the unemployment gap between young males and young females in most developed regions. In some of these countries, male-dominated industries were harder hit by the crisis (e.g. building construction).

[11] International Labour Organization, 2010, pp. 17-23
[12] International Labour Organization, 2011b, p. 10
[13] World Bank, 2010

YOUNG PEOPLE IN THE INFORMAL ECONOMY AND AMONG THE WORKING POOR

Most young workers in developing countries are in the informal economy, which includes unpaid family work to which young people often contribute.[14] Work in the informal economy does not provide access to entitlements such as health insurance, social security and other social protection measures. Workers tend to lack job and income stability such that any misfortune, for example, poor health or a natural disaster, can quickly lead to unemployment and falling into – or deeper into – poverty. Evidence points to increased rates of participation in the informal economy following the onset of the global economic crisis. An analysis of employment trends in six Latin American countries found that in 2009, up to 82.4 per cent of young people between the ages of 15 and 19 were employed in the informal economy, up from 80.8 per cent in 2007, and compared to 50.2 per cent of adults between the ages of 30 and 64.[15]

Informal employment falls outside the reach of government regulation, and is therefore more susceptible to exploitative conditions. In fact, the period between 2004 and 2008 saw a 20 per cent rise in the number of young people between the ages of 15 and 17 who were engaged in hazardous work – work that is harmful to their health and personal development. In 2008, nearly half of young workers in that age group were in such employment, which affects more than twice as many boys as girls.[16]

"Working poverty" defined

According to the International Labour Organization: A measure of people who work but live in households in which income/expenditure is less than US$1.25 per person a day.

---

[14] International Labour Organization, 2010, p. 3
[15] International Labour Organization, Regional Office for Latin America and the Caribbean, 2009, p. 52. Global Employment Trends for Youth: Special issue on the impact of the global economic crisis on youth. Geneva: International Labour Office, p. 39.
[16] International Labour Organization, International Programme on the Elimination of Child Labour, 2011, pp. 7-9

About 152 million young workers live in households that are below the poverty line of the equivalent of US$1.25 per day – comprising 24 per cent of the total working poor.[17] Working poverty thus affects approximately twice the number of young people world-wide than does unemployment, despite the alarming rate of youth unemployment. Many of the working poor are engaged in agricultural work in countries and regions where unemployment rates are relatively low, such as in South Asia, East Asia and sub-Saharan Africa, yet where there is limited access to social protection. Young workers who are trapped in working poverty – who represent 28.1 per cent of all young workers, globally[18] – may be unable to pursue an education that could offer them better quality employment opportunities in the future. Without such opportunities, prospects for a better life for them and their children remain dim.

WHAT YOUNG PEOPLE SAY

What are the important positive and negative employment trends among youth that you have observed in your community/ country?

REGIONAL/GEOGRAPHICAL CHALLENGES

- Young people from several regions echoed the research revealing that young people are disproportionately affected by employment challenges. Nikola, 24, a young man from Croatia who works with the Croatian Youth Network, wrote about his country: *"The situation is currently really bad [...] The overall unemployment rate has risen [since] 2008, and resulted in 283,667 registered unemployed persons. This is in a country with 4,290,612 people [...] Generally speaking, the youth unemployment rate rose much faster than the overall unemployment rate [...] you have a high number of skilled and trained people in the labour market with experience, and employers would normally first employ those people with experience rather then young inexperienced youths."*

- A large number of participants expressed frustration with such growing job competition due to high unemployment, resulting in what they feel are unattainable job requirements. This was described clearly by Georgina, 25, from the United Kingdom: *"The job market in the [United Kingdom] UK is becoming increasingly competitive. In the past, a Bachelor's degree was enough to set one apart in certain employment sectors. Nowadays, young graduates are expected to possess a Master's in addition to several years of work experience in order to obtain an entry level position."* To this, Parth, a 24-year-old male from India, added a concern shared by many

[17] International Labour Organization, 2010, p. 26
[18] ibid.

participants, that those young people who are able to find a job must take it at: *"an extremely low salary. Some employers are using this as an opportunity to exploit youth."*

- Lody, 25, from Cambodia, shared her view of the reasons for higher unemployment among youth than adults in her country: *"[...] lack of quality of education, [lack of] skills among students and job seekers, skills mismatch between what students have acquired in schools and the skills needed by employers, lack of networking at the workplace, poor work experience and workplace skills, etc."* These reasons were frequently cited by many other participants. Amadou, 24, from Senegal, working with AFRIC'Action, pointed out the irony of such factors given that today's generation of young people is in fact the most educated.

- The severity of young people's precarious and insecure work situation, and the frustration it is causing, was captured by Leo, a 28-year-old from Spain:

"Currently, 20 per cent of our [total] active population is unemployed. We can blame the economic crisis, our government, or our economic structure [...] youth is particularly affected. We finished our studies and we jumped into a job market full of insecurities [...] Jobs for young people are miserable in Spain. If you find one you are more than lucky, but then problems start:

- They want you to be young, smart, have five years of undergraduate education, a Master's degree, three languages, four years of experience, etc [...] but they pay you around 850 euros per month. Because of the economic crisis, companies try to reduce costs and increase productivity at the same time. Productivity is transformed into stress [for] the employee. The employee [is] constantly afraid because of the threat of losing her/his job.

- Contracts are very restrictive – normally, [there are] six to 12 months on probation. Within that time the employer can fire anyone without giving more explanation than: 'your services are not required anymore in order to fulfil our objectives.' Young people have this kind of contract and that's the reason why they cannot even pay for their own houses, because banks don't give loans if you have unstable contracts.

- So, when one almost reaches the end of the probation period. Surprise!!!!! You are fired."

- Contributors from developing countries, and in particular from Africa, mentioned that corruption and preferential family and political connections pose a disadvantage to most youth, as only those people who are well placed in society appear to have access to decent jobs. Walter, 18, from Lagos, Nigeria believes that: *"In Nigeria, the main cause of unemployment is corruption, which is having a negative effect on virtually all sectors in my country."* Similarly, Thulani from Zimbabwe expressed: *"It is a very unfortunate situation that those who benefit are those who have political connections with dominant political parties."*

Although Anna, 30, from Kenya, found that the government sector offered better working conditions to youth than the private sector, she appealed for more action on the parts of both government and youth to improve the youth employment situation:

"Young people in the labour market in Kenya is a critical issue. Young people are exploited and subjected to very harsh working conditions, poor pay, and too large workloads. Sometime I feel pity, yet [there is] nothing I can do about it, most companies are foreign owned and private. The government side, as much as people criticize, I would testify that it offers better packages to young people, and even job security, and the working environment is favourable. It's in this spirit that we encourage the government to open up more opportunities for young people in order for the private sector to wake up to the call. My other concern is that we young people should come out of comfort zones and start fighting for our space in all sectors of our respective countries. Rather than sit back and cry foul at our [...] States and governments, we should shape our future, get into leadership positions and influence policies and decision-making organs directly."

This call was echoed by Shayla, 25, of the United States, who urged: *"Youth not only need an opportunity to train to be better leaders, but also the opportunity to be leaders."*

MIGRATION

Participants expressed mixed views on labour migration, both internal – which, in most cases, is rural to urban – and international. Many young people viewed migration as a source of opportunity and hope, representing the "pull factors." Several experiences showed that migration can indeed lead to improved job prospects.

Internal migration is typically associated with the growth of cities and industries that is representative of national economic growth and development. Increased agricultural productivity generally reduces reliance on the agricultural sector and gives way to greater investment in and expansion of the industrial sector, which tends to be concentrated in urban areas. Therefore, although it does not always lead to decent work, rural to urban migration can be an indicator of healthy economic growth. One participant shared that those with education and skills in rural Kenya seek jobs in cities such as Nairobi and Mombasa where, in comparison to villages, resources and incomes are better and opportunities are easily available.

International migration tended to be viewed by participants as a potential solution to the effects of the economic crisis on employment. Leo, 28, from Spain wrote of his views on international migration: *"We, the youth, we are losing hope. We try to blame others expecting that one day everything will be fine, that one day someone will knock on our door offering us the job of our dreams [...] but why do we have to wait? We need to innovate, to risk, to create, to search [...] why not in another country, for example?"*

• At the same time, participants tended to highlight the "push" factors of internal and international migration, representing the poor conditions in young people's places of origin that lead them to consider migrating for work. They expressed concern for the long-term impacts of migration on such places of origin, which risk persistent under- development. Emad, 28, from Egypt, working with Etijah, Youth & Development Consultancy Institute, illustrated these issues with particular reference to rural areas: *"I grew up in a small village in the south of Egypt. When I graduated from university, I found that job opportunities were so limited and that most of the well-educated graduates leave to the Arabian Gulf countries, to big cities or to Cairo, which in turn keeps the rural regions less developed and affects the quality of life."*

Sebastian from Romania conveyed a similar message regarding emigration from his country: *"Take for example Romania, where I live. It is a country where young people cannot easily settle for a job [...] because the country has no good policy for youth employment. There are not enough economic reasons for the young to settle in the country (salaries are too low to make a living or to finance a family), and thus they tend to go abroad for low-level, non-professional jobs that give them a better life/economic expectations. I think the government should [develop] policies that reward young people who start careers in their home locations, and they also should be motivated for local development. No one wants to leave home, and that is why those who get the chance to be motivated at work, not only – but at least – with money (to have a decent living), will remain and help with local development, which will lead to national development and so on."*

• Other participants mentioned the difficulty they, or someone they know, were facing abroad. For instance, some young migrants have had to accept jobs with low salaries and for which they were overqualified because their university degrees were not accepted in the host country. Joseph from Latvia also pointed to the effects of migration on families:

"My brother and his family migrated to [the United Kingdom] UK and now they have found a 'normal life' [...] Now I see them not more than once a year. But I am happy for them."

• "Brain-drain" is also a concern for youth, for example the rural to urban migration from the Out Islands to the capital city/island in the Bahamas and externally to larger countries. The issues was also identified in Nepal, about which Ashesh wrote: *"In a poor economy like Nepal, there is an acute shortage of skilled youths [...] Unemployment of the skilled ones is pushing them to the long queues in front of every manpower consultancy to seek jobs in foreign countries."*

POSITIVE SIGNS FOR YOUTH EMPLOYMENT

● Despite the largely negative employment landscape portrayed by participants, there were some flickers of hope. Lody, 25, from Cambodia, shared what her job meant to her:

"I have been employed with good working conditions and a decent wage. My family's living conditions are also rising. My job has changed my life, and I try my best to overcome and struggle through any challenges facing me and my family. Those challenges are high food prices, a high cost of living [...] and a sustainable livelihood."

However, Lody continued on to express that her: *"job is somehow not secure at all, and I need to be well prepared for another job whenever I am told I will be redundant [...] The labour market is very competitive, so we need to earn more experience and degrees to adapt to the requirements."*

● Some participants pointed to governmental or civil society programmes designed to improve young people's employment opportunities. Ayshah, 26, wrote about her town in the coastal region of Kenya, where young people are accessing organizations that provide skills training and volunteering assignments. *"[...] Young people are engaging themselves in forming groups that will enable them [...] to identify job opportunities in the community [...] We are advocating for young people to be job creators and not job seekers."*

● Emad, 28, from Egypt cited the recent political uprising in his country to illustrate the importance of good governance to youth empowerment:

"The revolution in Egypt, that is led by frustrated but hopeful youth, is stimulated by a long history of failure to solve the unemployment problem, corruption and human rights violations. We revolt with a hope that once we have a good governance system, Egypt will attract more investments and jobs [...] There is a strong connection between security and economic and social empowerment, with a young generation understanding that close relationship and fighting for securing both."

How are young people participating and adding value to achieving decent work/jobs for all in your city/town/locality?

● Entrepreneurship was a recurrent theme during the week I discussions, including with regard to contributing or adding value to the achievement of decent work. Young people pursue entrepreneurship either out of preference or, increasingly, out of necessity in cases where they are unable to find other work. Several participants strongly felt that youth entrepreneurship is a promising solution to rising or persistent unemployment. There were many calls for greater opportunities to develop skills that are needed for entrepreneurial activities, including in schools. Hawawu, a 27-year-old woman from Ghana, stated:

"What we need is to be able to develop our entrepreneurial skill and abilities, so that instead of us waiting to be employed, we can create jobs for ourselves and employ others, to [...] entrepreneurship alone might be the solution; other skill development areas such as vocational, technical and business skills could [also] be exploited. Further, our educational curricula must be designed to bridge the gap already created by our system of education, especially in Africa."

ON THE UPSIDE

● Many participants remarked that, in recent years, the number of successful youth entrepreneurs has risen. Positive examples of youth entrepreneurship were cited in several countries, including the Bahamas, Kenya and Cambodia. In some cases, such as the Young Entrepreneurs Association of Cambodia, young entrepreneurs gather together and share their experiences and lessons learned.

ON THE DOWNSIDE

● Ayshah, 26, from Kenya also pointed out that *"not everybody is an entrepreneur."* Participants acknowledged that some aspects of entrepreneurial talent, such as risk- taking, cannot be developed with training or resources. They indicated that it is very difficult to create a new business from scratch, including due to the sometimes limited availability of credit among young people as well as to a lack of trust and confidence in them. In fact, most participants who were themselves young entrepreneurs mentioned that they had inherited their business from their parents. In this way, it remains a family business and is thus considered self-employment. Given the risks inherent to entrepreneurship, and recognizing that it does not always lead to decent and productive work, self-employment – in the words of Nikola, 24, from Croatia – may be viewed as *"one of the solutions."*

● Frank, 26, from the United States, with the organization, World Faith, shared a cautiously optimistic view of youth entrepreneurship:

"I'd be interested in hearing more about how we can encourage youth entrepreneurship in the face of a bad economy. Historically, entrepreneurship has created new employment opportunities, but in the current economy, there are external factors, like industry protections, and internal factors, like high student debt, that seem to be curtailing the entrepreneurial instinct."

FINAL INSIGHTS

● In many cases, participants rather commented on their frustration with not being able to contribute more towards decent work. Jasmin, 17, from Malaysia observed during the e-discussion that there seemed to be *"more negative employment trends [...] than positive. I'm sure everyone here hopes for better."* Others remarked that it should be easier for young people to find work, earn respect and live decently.

● Numerous comments shared by participants revealed a sense of neglect on the part of governments to the youth employment challenge, and worried about the implications for young people's potential. Sandra from Slovenia wrote: *"[...] everything seems good on paper, but unfortunately [...] governments don't do a lot to implement ideas [...] just think about how many young people there are in the world with huge potential, who could actually implement so many ideas but because of some reason the chances are not given to us [...] It's like they are not interested in making the situation better [...]"*

What are the up-and-coming areas for youth employment in your country?

● The sector in which participants continue to find the greatest employment opportunities is that of information and communications technologies (ICTs). Some of the countries where jobs in ICT were referenced included Senegal, Latvia and Nigeria. Youssoupha, 23, from Senegal informed that: *"The young who have studied [information technology] IT, engineering, teaching and health don't face a lot of employment problems after graduation[...]the market lacks a workforce in these domains, so graduating in them offers you a great chance to have a job."*

● Enock, 29, shared that in his country of Uganda: *"Right now, we have very high unemployment among young college graduates with degrees in everything from health to technology. Trends seem to be in health-related fields, environmental studies and green development (energy)."*

● Participants expressed growing interest in the topic of green jobs. One young woman observed that many young people embrace the concept of "going green." Some, however, are hesitant to engage in this sector because it is an emerging one, despite its potential as an area for job creation. Paulo, 26, a volunteer with YMCA, shared the example of his country:

"Brazil discovered pre-salt in its coast, and needs green technology to [extract it] and to avoid environmental problems. As we [also] have one of the biggest forests in the world, youth and young students from some universities are preparing for the [expansion of] green jobs to increase our employment and youth employment rates."

● Zakita from the Bahamas observed growth in the area of eco-tourism in his country: *"As the main industry that we depend on, finding ways to attract people to the Bahamas in a sustainable way while having a better appreciation of nature and the environment is something that has gained credibility."*

YOUTH EMPLOYMENT CHALLENGES ALSO PRESENT SOCIAL RISKS

Decent work deficits have a range of social and other implications. Increasingly, young people are moving to cities or migrating to countries with greater job opportunities, separating from their families and social support networks.[19] Along with migration comes a risk of exploitation and trafficking, particularly among vulnerable youth. Lack of decent work additionally affects well-being, frequently creating frustration and discouragement, which risk triggering more severe mental health problems such as depression, strained family relations, and even contributing to anti-social behaviours such as drug abuse.[20] Poor working conditions also lead to a variety of minor to serious physical and mental health issues.

Youth employment challenges further influence social institutions and processes such as marriage and parenthood for young people. In response to their employment situation, there is some evidence that young people are delaying marriage and pregnancy, adjusting family size and assuming increased caregiving responsibilities. Many young people are also moving back home with family or sharing homes to cut expenses.[21]

WHAT YOUNG PEOPLE SAY

Youth employment and well-being — what have been the positive/negative impacts of your job on your family life?

● The linkages between youth employment and a country's social, economic as well as political health were aptly highlighted in the post-conflict context of Sierra Leone by Bob, who works with the National Secondary School News Network Youth Desk:

"The employment of youth [...] has positive implications for economic growth, political stability and national security. On the other hand, youth unemployment has negative implications likely to result in economic downturns, political instability, national insecurity and a high possibility of reversals in peace gains since the war ended in 2002. Understanding the state of Sierra Leone's

[19] International Labour Organization, 2011a, p.6
[20] International Labour Organization, 2010, p. 2
[21] This has recently been observed in the Middle East and North African region, in the United States and in the Republic of Korea. See Chamie, 2011; Kim, 2011; and Stobbe, 2011.

youth in terms of employment is therefore crucial to assessing the direction in which Sierra Leone is heading in peace gains and the transition from fragility to development."

● Participants widely identified the benefits of employment with independence in terms of leaving the home of their parents or other caregivers, both out of a sense of responsibility and with a view towards the possibility of starting a new family. They shared a common concern that high rates of unemployment *"discourage people from getting married because they won't have enough means to build a family – meaning enough money for health, paying government taxes, having children and taking care of their needs"* (Loubna, 23-year-old female, Morocco).

Another participant further expressed the desire to support his future children without total reliance on government social assistance.

Vote Corner

When you are looking for a job, will you choose a job based on your individual dreams or on the wishes of your family? Why?

Participants cast their votes on the International Year of the Youth Facebook page. The results were:

* Individual dreams (91 per cent of votes)
* Wishes of the family (9 per cent of votes)

Selection of responses from Facebook and Twitter:

@UNpYouth "I would choose my dream job because by living and fulfilling my dreams, I would not live in emptiness and regret it later in life."

@UNpYouth "Balance of both. I would only do something I love, but as a pretty trad[itional] Chinese, I'm consciously aware of looking after family."

Amel E.-B. answers "It is on my individual dreams not to the wishes of my family, but my family is in the centre of dreams and interests..."

Charles E. B. says "individual dreams definitely as the passion you have can allow you to grow while enhancing all efforts better."

- Joseph pointed out that in his country of Latvia, young people can find jobs, but: *"[...] with the minimal salary – 230 euros that is standard for 40 per cent of vacancies – it is impossible to live normally, because you even cannot afford to rent a flat; maybe it is enough to rent a room, but a person needs to buy food, clothes, etc. And you cannot afford a child, to make a family. That's why many people aged 18-25 leave our country. [...] I want to live like a person."*

Andrew painted a similar – yet even more stark – picture of the situation in his country, Rwanda: *"The employment of most youth in developing countries has little impact on their lives, because most of the youth come from poor families; when one gets a job [...] the starting of a new family becomes a problem. Secondly, youth depend on low-paid jobs which may not allow them to meet all [of their] basic needs."*

- Amadou, 24, from Senegal revealed that while young men in his country prefer to have a job before marriage because they are expected to be providers, and are getting married later in life, educated young women are also choosing to do the same *"[...] because they want to be more independent. Personally, I think the same. I don't want to get married until I am financially independent. It could have negative effects on a couple's well-being."*

YOUNG PEOPLE ARE A DIVERSE SOCIAL GROUP

WHAT THE RESEARCH SHOWS

Young workers are not a homogenous group. There are certain social groups that face distinct disadvantages which, intersecting with the social exclusion experienced by youth, broaden the challenge of their finding opportunities for decent work. In general, young women have more difficulty in securing decent work opportunities; in 2010, the global unemployment rate for young females was 12.9 per cent, compared with 12.5 per cent for young males. Unemployment rates for young women in the Middle East and North Africa are nearly twice as high as those of young men; almost 40 per cent of all young women in the Middle East were unemployed in 2010. By contrast, in the developed economies and the European Union and in East Asia, young men have experienced slightly higher unemployment rates than young women.[22]

[22] International Labour Organization, 2011b, p. 10

The very young in most countries also face difficulty in securing decent work opportunities. Unemployment rates among ethnic minorities tend to be higher. Indigenous youth and youth with disabilities often deal with multiple forms of discrimination and face major specific obstacles when seeking employment. The level of education itself can be a factor leading to unemployment depending on the economic conditions prevailing in a country. In developed countries, unemployment is higher among less educated people, while in developing countries, unemployment tends to be high among more educated youth, leading to the problem of educated unemployment.[23]

WHAT YOUNG PEOPLE SAY:

● Participants identified the most vulnerable youth as girls and young women, youth from poor families, unskilled youth and rural youth. This determination was linked to each participant's region, such as rural or urban, as well as country and cultural context. For instance, girls and young women are frequently disadvantaged in the labour market, even if change is underway and more opportunities are opening to them. Lody, 25, shared that options for youth in the labour market of her country, Cambodia, were limited by the few industries and services of the mainly rural economy. Moreover, *"Young women are doubly affected as they face not only lack of opportunities, but poor quality of work, especially in the informal segments – characterized by low wages, less secure employment, and no voice representation."* However, Youssoupha, 23, from Senegal wrote that *"In the past, girls were also excluded from some jobs. But in recent years, they have been more and more favoured. So in some jobs proposals we often see "female candidates are encouraged to apply [...]"* Overall, Youssoupha observed that those:

"[...] who are facing a lot of difficulties in the job market are the rural youth. First of all, they are obliged to come to town if they want to have a proper education. And then as soon as they graduate they face other problems, too. Given the fact that they can't go back home and work (no jobs there), they don't have a choice but to stay in town and fill the ranks of unemployed people."

● Other groups of youth who were described by participants as marginalized from employment opportunities are young people without higher education as well as without connections to influential persons, including to access government contracts. Such groups were noted to likely be working in the informal sector. Roger from Ghana added that: *"In rural Ghana, the poor and vulnerable people are the youth who are the most likely to be the landless or small landowners (owning less than three hectares of cropland), small-scale artisans and traders [...]"*

● Amadou, 24, from Senegal brought participants' attention to an often overlooked group of young people: *"The marginalized are the young people living with disabilities. They face many problems in getting access to higher education because the infrastructure is not suitable to them, especially the buildings. So, when governments build schools or universities, they should think about people with disabilities."*

[23] International Labour Organization, 2011b, p. 21

A DIM OUTLOOK FOR YOUTH EMPLOYMENT

Countries continue to grapple with the effects of the global economic crisis, with many overburdened by massive debt. As a result, a growing number of governments are implementing austerity measures to reduce public spending, including in social sectors such as employment and education. Such measures involve laying off government workers and, in many cases, shrinking or even eliminating programmes that provide educational, health-related, job placement and other support and assistance to the public, particularly low-income and marginalized persons. Yet these financial cuts are occurring at precisely the same time when so many young people and other vulnerable groups of workers are most in need of social support. Moreover, there is evidence to demonstrate that austerity programmes themselves can lead to increases in unemployment levels.

Previous economic recessions have shown that youth employment conditions recover much more slowly than resumptions of economic growth. In the 1990s, countries required an average of 11 years to restore pre-crisis lows of youth unemployment.[24] Those countries that were not able to restore pre-crisis levels took, on average, 17 years to attain a partial recovery. During recovery phases, displaced workers who found new jobs generally earned lower wages. These lessons from previous crises suggest that youth employment challenges are likely to persist for some time.

CONCLUSIONS

In general terms, the comments shared by participants in the e-discussion on youth employment confirmed what is stated in various reports on the topic; young people are facing various employment challenges, reflected in insecure employment, high unemployment and other measures. Youth are broadly concerned that there are too few opportunities for decent work. They are worried about the prevalence of unemployment, inadequate and falling salaries and poor working conditions; poor quality education, lack of skills, and skills ill-adapted to labour market needs; gender and other inequalities; the risks and benefits associated with labour migration; independence and the fulfilment of aspirations for marriage and parenthood; and governmental support for improving the situation of youth employment.

One particular aspect of young people's contributions to the e-discussion can be linked to recent social and political movements across the world: the hopelessness of youth regarding what they perceive as their countries' lack of prioritization of their concerns as well as institutional capacity to address them. Young people shared the sense that they have been left to fend for themselves. This was clearly described by Bob, 24, from Sierra Leone:

[24] International Labour Organization, International Institute for Labour Studies, 2010, Box 1.1

"The reason for the unemployment of young people in any nation is the fact that they are not prioritized by their government. Youth are to be seen as leaders of today in any nation for [it...] to be able to fully address the issues of development and unemployment. But instead, [they have] always been referred to 'As the future leaders of tomorrow'. With this, youths will not be able to fully participate in designing programmes to address the unemployment rates in their countries. The solution to this problem will only be the young people themselves, because they know their problems and, if allowed to discuss them frankly in the presence of those concerned, society will appreciate them and look out for adequate solutions..."

Participants expressed considerable frustration and, in some cases, detachment from the labour market and a loss of hope. Among the youngest of all participants, Mridula, a 16-year-old girl from India, was pessimistic about her future opportunities:

"[...] I'm a high school student and hence, do not need a job right now. However, I cannot close my eyes and let an issue of this magnitude go unnoticed. The youth of a country are its future. What is the use of education if we are not given a chance to put our knowledge and skills into work? I have to admit that India is one of the countries in which the youth, even those with good degrees, are unemployed. They are not given a chance to start working because employers prefer experienced men. How are we supposed to gain experience if we are not even presented with an opportunity to start working?"

Finding and motivating young people who have given up hope for a productive future is an expensive venture. Nonetheless, when the social, economic and potential political costs are considered, the alternative of doing nothing is even more expensive.

CASE STUDY
Emad, 28-year-old man from Egypt

Since I was 8 years old, I have had a dream to work in socio-economic development. Growing up in a small village in the south of Egypt, such a career was more like a fancy than a reachable dream.

After high school, I studied education with a vision of reform. Yet my school's main goal was to mass produce teachers, regardless of teacher quality or the market's need for them. Large numbers of unprepared teachers compete for limited temporary positions, perpetuating a cycle of low-quality education in the public education sector. Moreover, low salaries and instability of jobs have forced most of my colleagues to take on second jobs, in addition to teaching. Not willing to be part of this cycle, I had to either change my career or, at least, to take a different route than teaching alone.

Fewer opportunities exist for work in education in the southern regions of Egypt than in Cairo and other big cities. With no access to student loans in the country, I was lucky to have the support of my family in order to go to graduate school for an advanced specialized degree. Yet the graduate programme was, again, too broad and theoretical to foresee its practical implications. However, in 2005, the government supported a trend to prepare more information and communication technology (ICT) cadres for a demanding market by training graduate students who were willing to change their careers. In preparation for a career in developing ICT solutions for education, I decided to study software development for one year. The graduate degree and technological training and certificates, together, gave me better chances for a good job than any of my undergraduate colleagues had. Unfortunately, though, I had to move from the southern village where I grew up to seek work elsewhere that matched my new skills and aspirations.

In 2008, I noticed a growing tendency to hire graduates of international schools for policymaking and other higher-level positions. For a young southern youth from an under-privileged community, it is hard to afford such high-quality education in a well recognized international graduate school, but I was fortunate to get a scholarship to study at New York University in the United States. The degree I earned from that university, as well as internship experience I gained during my studies, qualified me for a senior-level job in a youth and development consultancy institute in Egypt, allowing me to realize my dream.

Working in the development field now, it is ironic for me to see the effects of development on social movement in the south, as qualified youth migrate to metropolitan areas. Yet I also see how I can help to serve my home village and similar villages. The disparity between the South and North (in national and international scope) will continue to exist for some time, depriving a lot of youth from the South of opportunities to grow, and forcing them to take extra steps in order to be as qualified as those from the North. However, with determination, improved education, equal opportunities and guidance, southern youth can play more effective roles in developing their communities.

CURRENT FACTS ABOUT YOUTH DEMOGRAPHICS WORLDWIDE[25]

Globally, the number of young people rose to 1.21 billion in 2010, from 461 million in 1950. The number of young people worldwide will increase only slightly by 2050, to 1.25 billion (medium variant).

Today, the Asian region has the largest number of young people: 754 million. That number has nearly tripled since 1950.

The African region had 205 million young people in 2010. However, that number

[25] United Nations, Department of Economic and Social Affairs, Population Division, 2011

has quintupled since 1950. By year 2100, the number is expected to increase to 505 million – such that the region will have the largest number of young people.

The countries with the largest number of young people in 2010 include: India, China and the United States.

The countries with the current highest percentage of young people in 2010 include: Swaziland, Zimbabwe and the Maldives.

CURRENT FACTS ABOUT GIRLS AND YOUNG WOMEN[26]

Among 14- to 19-year-old girls and young women, 42 per cent in South Asia, and 26 per cent in sub-Saharan Africa, are neither studying nor in paid employment – stuck in the transition from school to work.

In all regions, by the age of 24, young women's labour force participation trails young men's.

RESOURCES

United Nations, Department of Economic Affairs, Division for Social Policy and Development. Youth resources and publications.
http://social.un.org/index/Youth/ResourcesandPublications.aspx

Youthpolicy.org. Employment.
http://www.youthpolicy.org/

Network for Youth in Transitions. Employment.
http://networkforyouthintransition.org/forum/categories/youth-and-livelihood/listForCategory

Outcomes of the Hungarian Presidency European Union Youth Conference on youth employment; Budapest, 2-4 March 2011.
http://eu2011.mobilitas.hu/userfiles/file/Outcomes%20Budapest%20EU%20Youth% 20Conference.pdf

Global Entrepreneurship Monitor
http://www.gemconsortium.org/default.aspx
International Labour Organization. Decent work for Africa's youth.
http://bit.ly/nxAXeT

[26] World Bank (2010)

ADDITIONAL RESOURCES

Coy, Peter (2011). The youth unemployment bomb. Bloomberg Business week, 2 February. Available from http://www.businessweek.com/magazine/content/11_07/b4215058743638.htm

Garcia, Marito and Jean Fares, Eds. (2008). Youth in Africa's labour market. Directions in Development – Human Development. Washington, D.C.: World Bank.

Ha Byung-jin, Caroline McInerney, Steven Tobin and Raymond Torres (2010). Youth employment in crisis. Discussion Paper, No. 201. Geneva: International Labour Organization, International Institute for Labour Studies.

InterAction (2011). Monday Developments Magazine, vol. 29, No. 8 (August): http://www.interaction.org/document/youth-make-themselves-heard

International Labour Organization (2011). Global Wage Report 2010/2011: Wage policies in times of crisis. Geneva: International Labour Office.

International Labour Organization (2011). Growth, employment and decent work in the least developed countries. Report of the International Labour Office for the Fourth Conference on the Least Developed Countries, Istanbul, 9-13 May 2011.

Matsumoto, Makiko and Sara Elder (2010). Characterizing the school-to-work transitions of young men and women: Evidence from the ILO school-to-work transition surveys. Employment Working Paper, No. 51 (June). Geneva: International Labour Office.

United Nations Economic and Social Commission for Western Asia (2010). Youth development in the ESCWA region: statistical profiles, national strategies and success. 14 April. Available from http://www.escwa.un.org/information/publications/edit/upload/sdd-10-B1.pdf

World Bank (2008). The economic participation of adolescent girls and young women: why does it matter? Washington, D.C.: World Bank. http://siteresources.worldbank.org/INTGENDER/Resources/morrison_sabarwal08.pdf

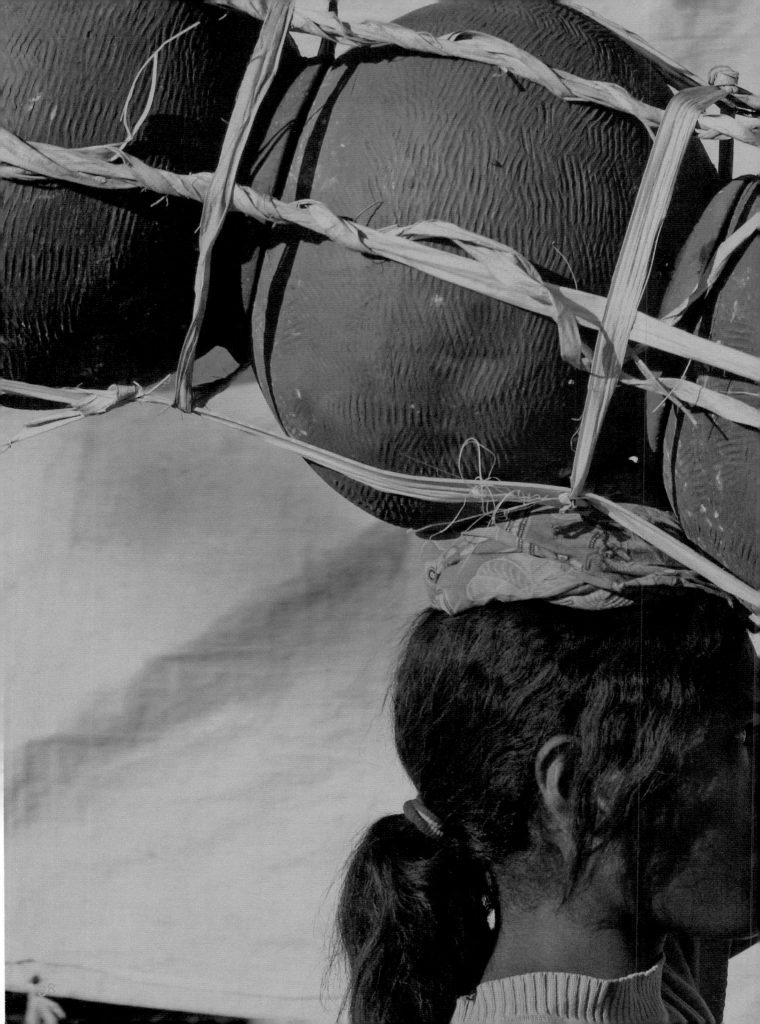

How can we not only create **skills** that match the labour market, but also **quality jobs** that match the **aspirations of young people**?"
-Steffi, 29

UN Photo/Martine Perret
September 2007 | Timor-Leste

CHAPTER II

PREPARING FOR WORK

RELEVANT HIGHER EDUCATION – LET'S FOCUS!

Education can take many forms. These include: formal education (through academic mainstream schooling, including technical and vocational instruction for youth[1]); informal education (learning that takes place outside of institutions); special education (for those experiencing intellectual/physical disability); and non-formal education (life-relevant knowledge and skills acquired both within and outside educational institutions).

According to the United Nations Educational, Scientific and Cultural Organization, during the adolescent years it is formal education which is "the most effective base for developing learning and life skills".[2] Furthermore, while the number of adolescents outside the formal education system – just under 74 million in 2008 – has been declining, there are large regional variations. Secondary education suffers from particularly high levels of global inequality. Most rich countries are close to universal secondary school enrolment, while developing countries lag behind.[3]

Education for All Global Monitoring Report 2011: secondary and tertiary education statistics

Sub-Saharan Africa has registered rapid increases in secondary school coverage. Enrolment ratios have increased by 40 per cent since 1999 – the most rapid growth rate in the world. Mozambique has increased secondary enrolment five-fold.

Despite these impressive increases, youth in sub-Saharan Africa are half as likely to be in secondary school as youth in the Arab States.

Secondary school attendance and completion are strongly influenced by poverty, location and gender. People aged 23 to 27 in Cambodia from the wealthiest 20 per cent of households have secondary completion rates of 28 per cent, compared with 0.2 per cent for the same age group from the poorest households.

[1] While technical and vocational enrolment has increased in most regions globally, there are significant variations; with central and eastern Europe having the largest percentage (19 per cent) of secondary school students enrolled (United Nations, Educational, Scientific and Cultural Organization, 2011a).
[2] United Nations, Educational, Scientific and Cultural Organization, 2011a, p. 54
[3] ibid.

Tertiary education has been expanding world-wide, with 65 million more students enrolled in 2008 than in 1999. Much of the growth has occurred in East Asia and the Pacific, with China alone increasing the number of tertiary places by more than 20 million.

The upshot is that already large global disparities in tertiary enrolment ratios are widening.[4]

Although access to formal education is extremely important, it is equally important to focus on quality; how effective it is. This is particularly significant in the increasingly skills-based global economy, where "higher [secondary/tertiary/vocational] education systems play a vital role in skills development".[5] Unfortunately, here too, there are large global inequalities, and some of the gaps are widening. The Education for All Global Monitoring Report 2011 states that, "Access to tertiary education is expanding more rapidly in richer than in poorer countries. Left unchecked, this development is likely to have major implications for future patterns of economic growth and globalization".[6]

Indeed, the Africa Youth Report 2011[7] emphasizes that, "A critical analysis of the current education situation in the region has led stakeholders to believe that there seems to be an overemphasis on enrolment numbers rather than attendance and the relevance of education." This sentiment was also echoed by the majority of the participants in the e-discussion on youth employment.

High-quality multifaceted education has a positive impact on decent jobs. This was highlighted at the 7th Youth Forum of the United Nations Educational, Scientific and Cultural Organization (UNESCO) held in Paris from 17 to 20 October 2011. The 7th UNESCO Youth Forum final report[8] acknowledges the correlation between practical education and ever evolving employment needs, whereby a recommendation for Education, no. 8, states:

"In response to employment challenges, we strongly encourage Member States to expand the scope of education by including entrepreneurial skills and training opportunities, and intergenerational partnerships for youth aligned to rapidly changing labour market needs, particularly in non-traditional fields, such as e-learning."

Furthermore, the Young Foundation encouraged readers to look past the headlines and take the time to listen, understand and act. A representative of the Foundation, Gemma Rocyn-Jones, reported that:

[4] Source: United Nations, Educational, Scientific and Cultural Organization, Institute for Statistics, Data Centre (UIS database).
[5] The Education for All Global Monitoring Report 2011 (ibid.)
[6] The Education for All Global Monitoring Report 2011 (ibid.)
[7] United Nations, Economic Commission for Africa, 2011
[8] United Nations, Educational, Scientific and Cultural Organization, 2011b

"The key recommendations of [a 2011 publication] The Way to Work: Young People Speak Out on Transitions to Employment [(Kahn, Abdo, Hewes and others, 2011)] were echoed [...] in a report on global unemployment trends by the International Labour Organization. This has called for education and training to improve its relevance to labour market needs and for broad-based partnerships between everyone who plays a role in a young person's transition to employment, including employers. Perhaps it is time for everyone to move past the headlines, stop talking at each other and start listening so that expectations and aspirations can become aligned".[9]

Indeed, this call was further echoed by participants on the e-discussion platform: let us start listening and collaborating in a meaningful way.

WAKE UP: QUALITY EDUCATION GOES HAND IN HAND WITH DECENT WORK

From 18 to 24 October 2011, week II, the e-discussion platform was open to all to discuss the realities of how their education systems have prepared them (and their peers) to access employment. There were more than 300 comments posted by young people from more than 95 countries across the globe – including from Peru, Senegal, Kenya, Yemen and India. Although the e-discussion invited the views of young people aged 15 to 30,[10] as well as representatives of youth-led organizations, comments during week II were received from young people between the ages of 19 and 29. Therefore, the present chapter may not capture the views of all adolescents. In addition, there were at least 845 people (ages unknown) who accessed and viewed the platform during the week.

This chapter explores education in its broadest sense, as the foundation for working life, with a focus on views regarding educational quality and relevance to labour markets. While some positive comments were shared, the overall consensus was that many educational systems and institutions around the world are still insufficiently tailored and aligned to the dynamic needs of the labour market. As Bwenje, a young Ugandan states, *"instead of training young people to seek jobs, they should train students to create jobs."*

[9] Rocyn-Jones, 2011
[10] This is taking into account both the United Nations definition of youth (15- to 24-year-olds) and many local cultural contexts and understandings.

WHAT YOUNG PEOPLE SAY:

How well do you think that your formal academic or training institution has prepared you for decent jobs?

ON THE UPSIDE

● Several participants from Asia, the Caribbean and the Middle East shared positive experiences as foreign students studying at universities abroad. Yasmyn, 24, from Guadeloupe (currently studying in Canada), said that in comparison (to her home country), *"young people here [in Montreal] are highly trained."* Sara, from Yemen, who studied at the American University in Dubai, went further to say that she found her communication course *"extremely practical and hands on."* They both agreed that they felt well prepared to find a job once they completed their studies.

● Rishabh, 21, from India and several others also noted that the experience of finding a job back in their home country was, however, easier than in the country where they had studied.

● There was debate amongst young Indians as to the quality of tertiary education in their country. Kirthi, 24, from India, however, noted that as an emerging economy, India has a:

"Fairly well-balanced education system [...] most of our colleges are well-equipped with curricula that offer both practical and theoretical knowledge, in the form of both course study and internship options that help students understand the exact demands of their chosen paths. Medical school requires a mandatory house residency that teaches students hands on, law and engineering schools require students to take up internships."

ON THE DOWNSIDE

● Posts such as this one from Dayo, 26, in Nigeria were common: *"My academic training did not prepare me for paid employment at all. I cannot still believe that we were taught programming languages that were not in use any more like Pascal, Cobol, and the like (I did computer/ mathematics). We had to read and pass, not read to understand and apply."*

● The general consensus was that *"academic institutions are focused too much on theoretical learning, and not enough on practical skills"* (Ivan, 26, with the Youth Section of the Union of Autonomous Trade Unions of Croatia). Ivan went on to say:

"Schools are not equipping young people with some of the skills required for employment such as entrepreneurship, negotiation and networking skills. There is a lack of mentoring and guidance within schools on how to access employment. Only certain careers, such as medicine or law, seem to require practical experience to validate the final qualification."

● The frustration among participants was evident: Bijay, 27, from Nepal commented: *"The education in Nepal is producing educated unemployed youths. For example, last year I visited a rural district, Rolpa. The youth got vocational training; house wiring for young men and sewing for females, but only 5 per cent got a job or became self employed after."*

This example also illustrates the persistence of occupational sex segregation.

● Furthermore, several participants noted that the private and State employment sectors also need to collaborate more effectively with educational institutions (in order to communicate their needs). Schools and private enterprises lack coordinated and consistent linkages with each other, as Sanda_87 commented:

"Universities are not connected and do not cooperate with national and international companies in a way that provides their students with practical education, including how to work with people from different countries."

It is, however, important to note that this is not the case in all countries; one young Egyptian reported that there is a *"booming trend in Egypt from private institutions that are providing trainings to match careers [with] labour market trends."*

● Many participants also expressed frustration and even anger over the inequalities experienced in education systems across the globe. There remain great divides (particularly with regard to quality teaching) between private and public institutions. What is more, Emad, 28, from Egypt, working with Etijah, Youth & Development Consultancy Institute, observed that *"institutions also tend to push and support only the best students to access employment,"* and leave the ones who actually need the most support behind. Education is often only available for the best-off [...] and some young people with limited resources still find it difficult to access.

FINAL INSIGHTS

We were reminded by Matthieu Cognac, the International Labour Organization's Regional Specialist on Youth Employment in the Asia-Pacific region, (talking on the APYouthNet podcast) that, "obtaining degrees by itself is not an end to employability."

Instability and political unrest: Awa, 30, from Cameroon left all of us with a stark warning:

"Most students have no career guidance, no formal or informal trainings on CV/résumé development, job searching guidance, and interpersonal skills. With this mindset, youths find themselves confronted with the work world and its ever increasing challenges. The consequence among many is immediate frustration and desperation, and instead of serving as assets to their communities, they are instead liabilities. I say it is just a matter of time before the youth of most sub-Saharan African [countries] feel the multiplier effect of the Arab Spring."

In your country, what kinds of resources and services are available to support you and other young people in achieving your career aspirations?

ON THE UPSIDE

- Several of the participants from around the world acknowledged that their schools offered career guidance aimed at orienting students for the labour market, such as information on scholarships, trainings, internships and apprenticeships.

- Participants from India and Martinique cited the existence of educational fairs for students in their countries, whereby both schools/universities and the private sector (local businesses) shared information about opportunities and possible career paths available to young people. Some schools provide seminars and career guidance aimed at orienting students to the labour market, offering options for further scholarships, trainings, internships and apprenticeships.

- Several participants noted that their country had dedicated programmes for youth employment, such as the Plurinational State of Bolivia's "Programa Mi Primer Empleo Digno" (or My First Decent Employment Programme), and the National Employment Fund in Cameroon. Yet no one in this discussion appeared to have any direct involvement in these programmes.

- Many young participants were also interested in future employment opportunities within the United Nations. Hira, 23, with Y-Peer in Pakistan remarked that there were several opportunities, such as the United Nations Volunteers (UNV) Online Volunteering service, and that for her, getting country experience was important: *"that was when the doors opened for me!"*

ON THE DOWNSIDE

- Schools do provide support for students in the form of advisers/career guidance, but most participants shared the view that this is not enough. In addition, these support services are not available in every school.

- Even when resources and services exist, the lack of information about them prevents students from accessing them. These resources are also often only available for people who live in urban areas and/or come from wealthy families. Yanira, 29, from Colima, México told us that:

"According to a study of the Organization for Economic Cooperation and Development (OECD), Mexico ranks third with regard to the number of young people between 15 and 29 who neither work nor study. One root cause is that in my country there are large scholarship programmes from entry level to professional graduate/doctoral levels [...] I think it is very important to raise awareness and generate a host of actions for the benefit of all young people."

FINAL INSIGHTS

There were some interesting country examples of national youth employment funds, most notably, reported by Jose from the Dominican Republic. He commented on the strengths of the Institute of Professional Technical Formation (INFOTEP), which encourages and builds professional skills among students. In addition, the Dominican Republic also has a Youth and Employment Programme ("Juventud y Empleo") funded by the Inter-American Development Bank and the World Bank. Similarly, Cameroon has a National Employment Fund and Integrated Support Project for Informal Sectors (PIAASI).

Do you think that volunteerism and internships can adequately prepare young people for future paid employment? Do you have any personal examples to share?

ON THE UPSIDE

- Most participants believed that volunteering (2011 was the European Union Year of Volunteering) and internships are a vital part of an education: such opportunities make an individual stand out when seeking a job. Not only do they provide an *"opportunity to learn, but also an opportunity to put into practice new skills,"* says Seabe, 23, from Botswana. Thus, young people are able to familiarize themselves with a work environment and explore channels to network. Young people in this discussion all encouraged one another to get engaged in volunteerism and internships, with Bijay, 27, from Nepal concluding that, *"volunteerism has a double benefit: youth can develop their experience and skills and the government's development plan can be successful."*

Bob, 24, from Freetown in Sierra Leone told us: *"In my country, those young people benefitting from employment are those who are most connected to politicians. They will only create a short-term job for young people for a while, and later the whole thing will just die down [...] But there is an international organization called Restless Development that creates employment for young people through volunteerism and internships on a yearly basis. They have engaged a good number of youth who are just finishing their high school level of education."*

One participant from Yemen, Sara, explained how useful it was to start an internship while she was still studying. This allowed her to apply her studies, to boost her self-confidence and to make useful contacts:

"I would definitely encourage any young individual to go out and intern in different companies as much as they can. From my personal experience, doing internships while studying helped me to apply what I studied and implement it in the real world. These experiences boosted my confidence, and enhanced many aspects of my personality and social skills."

Edith, a third-year undergraduate from Ghana, confidently remarked that, *"I have plans to start my own media and graphic design company so I can also employ many Ghanaian youth. All of these opportunities and more that I cannot put on this page were a result of my interest in volunteering. I joined a media child rights advocacy group (Curious Minds) in 2001 as a volunteer when I was 11 years old. Most of the advocacy is done through regular radio programmes of national radio, quarterly magazines (the Springboard magazine), colloquiums, community outreach and outside broadcasts. Over the years, this experience exposed me to many issues and capacity-building sessions."*

ON THE DOWNSIDE

Internships can be used by employers as only a source for cheap labour. Internship conditions can be exploitative and do not always lead to employment, despite an intern's demonstrated skills and motivation. Seabe, age 23, from Botswana told us:

"I have submitted more than 80 CVs around the world in search of a job related to my degree, but I've had no luck. I remain hopeful though. Despite the internship programmes and trying to find

a job, I've been trying to get my own small business ventures started, but as I mentioned before, investors seem sceptical."

● The rural/urban divide was discussed among participants, several of whom highlighted that internships are often only available to the well-off and those living in urban areas. In addition, a lack of access to information about internship opportunities prevents young people from seizing them.

FINAL INSIGHTS

Internships/volunteering can foster social entrepreneurship [...] Tiburce, 26, from Benin (residing in India), who works with the Global Youth Innovation Network, told us:

"I created my own social business to help other young people to have a better understanding of what the marketplace requires. I am working on raising a new generation of African entrepreneurs. I wish the education system in African countries would integrate innovative advanced or complete solutions that help young people study and be an added value to the community. Theory should be 30 per cent and practice 70 per cent."

A challenge to us all from Tati: *"I think we need young people to be more proactive: we need to be linked up with research projects and volunteer opportunities in order to better understand the workplace."*

In your view, what role should vocational training play in preparing young people for the labour market? Does vocational training lead to stable and decent jobs?

Vocational training is being increasingly recognized as a sound mechanism to promote decent jobs. During week II of the e-discussion, the International Youth Foundation (IYF) launched the Tanzania Youth Scholars initiative. This initiative aims to increase access to quality vocational and entrepreneurship training and secondary education opportunities for 1,800 orphans and vulnerable children and young people through educational scholarships. The five-year programme is funded by the Emergency Plan for AIDS Relief (PEPFAR) of the President of the United States through that country's Agency for International Development (USAID). It's one to watch!

ON THE UPSIDE

● Eighty per cent of participants in the second week shared the view that vocational trainings are a very valid option for gaining practical work experience. They prepare trainees for jobs that are based on manual or practical activities, traditionally non-academic, and equip them with tangible relevant skills. One such example came from the Advanced Business Community (ABC), a student community established in 2007 at the faculty of commerce of Cairo University. Its aim is "to reduce the gap between the theoretical teachings at Egypt's commercial colleges and the practical world."

● One of the participants from Malindi in Kenya, 26-year-old Ayshah, informed us that, *"high school drop-outs"* present a big challenge in her town. According to Ayshah, *"the Digital Opportunity Trust (TOT), as well as [the United States Agency for International Development] USAID Aphia II Kenya initiative, offer training to marginalized youth who are trained as ambassadors of change [...] I have seen such training making a difference,"* she told us, *"in terms of them being role models and trying to find ways to sustain themselves in a positive manner."*

● Yasmyn, 24, from Guadeloupe informed us that, there: *"you get vocational training from the age of 16 and you get a diploma in practical skills 2-3 years later."* She commented that this is largely positive and that she has seen her peers grow more confident and independent because this system enables students to follow their chosen career paths, which may be outside of traditional curricula. She has seen peers, aged 18, securing employment in the vocations they studied.

● Germany was cited as a leading example in terms of integrating apprenticeships into education by Steffi, 29, from Germany. Typically, students enter a two- to three-year apprenticeship at the end of secondary education, with rotating periods between technical college and working in a company. Steffi went on to say that:

"The German model of apprenticeship programmes is the result of strong commitments negotiated through tripartite social dialogue and is part of the wider German industrial relations and social security system (the apprentice and employer contribute to the social security system and the apprentice is covered by wider collective agreements, etc.). So, in this case, vocational training can lead to decent employment. But with the increase in 'flexible' employment practices (outsourcing, etc.) and short-term orientation and economic transformations over the past decades, we can also witness a shift towards a two-tiered system for young workers in Germany: there are those who enter apprenticeships after school and will probably get a decent job, and those who are either unemployed or part of Germany's growing low-wage and precarious sector ("McJobs"). So, if we look at ideas for other countries, we need to take into account that vocational training is always part of a bigger employment picture, including cultural and political values and the wider economic structure."

ON THE DOWNSIDE

- Most participants shared the view that vocational trainings are not always easily available or accessible. Governments could do more to inform and reach out to diverse sections of youth populations.

- Vocational trainings are not always valued by employers. There remains some stigma, and they are often perceived as an opportunity for young people who do not have the capability to follow traditional academic pathways.

- Several participants commented that opportunities for vocational training (or access to information about them) remain limited and scarce, and that such training does not necessarily lead to decent and well-paid employment.

- Furthermore, Roger from Ghana told us that, "many young people, particularly the poorest, are starting work too early without the basic skills that could make them marketable. Students are completing secondary schools without having the skills that allow them to adapt to changes in the labour market."

FINAL INSIGHTS

Gaining vocational experience in a post-conflict environment...

Anna, 22, from the United States told us her story: *"In 2010, I had the opportunity to conduct research in Gulu, Uganda. While working in the area, I was able to gain a better understanding of the manner in which conflict impacted the community. The deep-seated impact of the war was visible not only in the economic and political spheres but also in the intangible, societal dynamics of the community. After working with several community members, however, I was also able to see the way in which the war highlighted the strength and determination of the community to recover from such far-reaching devastation. From that point forward, I decided to dedicate my studies to working with communities in conflict and reconciliation in order to help translate such resiliency into reconstruction. I also learned that, while grounding education in an academic context can be beneficial, experiential learning is also crucial to gain an accurate understanding of a situation or issue. I thus hope to continue my education by attempting to understand conflict from an academic standpoint while working to complement this knowledge base with real world experience."*

How do you view the role of non-formal education in job preparation? How has informal education influenced your job preparedness?

According to the United Nations Educational, Scientific and Cultural Organization (UNESCO), non-formal education refers to:

"Organized and sustained activities that take place both within and outside education institutions. Depending on country contexts, it may cover adult literacy, basic education for out-of-school children, life skills, work skills, and general culture. Non-formal education programmes do not necessarily follow the 'ladder' system, may have differing durations, and may or may not confer certification."

ON THE UPSIDE

- Many participants commented that non-formal education is an important part of their overall education, because it allows young people to acquire skills they would not normally access through formal education. Therefore, it is important for two reasons:

  1) It *"strengthens the skills of people who have been marginalized from formal education"* (said Charles, a young African); and
  2) It offers a different set of skills which are not provided through formal channels (Lauren, a young Latin American).

- One participant, Yasmyn, 24, from Guadeloupe commented that practicing cultural activities is also a good way of receiving informal education. She cited the example of attending traditional dances. This experience has benefited her in two ways:
  1) Teaching her about the history of her country; and
  2) Strengthening her transferable life skills in perseverance: *"these skills are really helping me now that I'm looking for an internship,"* she reports.

- For Ayshah, 26, from Kenya, her informal education has been through participating in seminars and trainings with young people who have a different background than hers, such as drug users.

Tweet Corner

From week II of the e-discussion

Uno de los problemas para elegir una carrera es la falta de información, según estudiantes http://t.co/Kp6xYhVq [One problem with choosing a career is the lack of information for students.]

RT @UNpYouth: [In Morocco, some people with a degree in any field don't even have the chance to find a decent internship] #youthjobs http://t.co/xqOiFmGv

RT @Rajdai: [Policymakers need 2 give alternatives 2 youth, n encourage #entrepreneurship n alternative careers] #youthjobs http://t.co/iTUvhunN@UNpYouth

ON THE DOWNSIDE

- According to some participants, non-formal education is not valued or recognized by some employers.

- In addition, Daniel, 28, from Switzerland and the United Kingdom and a member of the United Nations Youth Association Network (UNYANET), shared with us that:

"Non-formal education is important, but it sometimes lacks the option to actually prove what you have learned. This is connected to volunteering [...] if you learn how to organize a panel discussion for your association, by someone who has done it already, you will be able to organize it, but you will not be able to actually prove it - besides adding the 'flyer' to your application."

FINAL INSIGHTS

We are reminded that opportunities do exist to access non-formal education.

Angelica, with TDM 2000 International (a network of European youth organizations), told us:
"I would like to say that the European Union every year spends millions of euros in support of the education (formal and non-formal) and training of youth. There are many programmes, from Youth in Action to Life-Long Learning and to Erasmus for young entrepreneurs, and many, many more, that support financially the personal and professional development of young people. All of them are based on intercultural learning. I am not talking about the usual trainings in classrooms with teachers or experts – sure, you can find these as well – but mainly they are based on non-formal education, which is a well-established methodology that supports the learning of people of every age."

Are there any social/political/cultural factors which you perceive to be obstacles/challenges to your candidacy for employment? Can you provide any examples of overcoming such challenges?

- Many of the participants voiced their perceptions of age discriminatory practices across the labour market. Several commented on different forms of discrimination, including: age, gender, geography, nationality and ethnic background. Crispin, with Aube Nouvelle pour la Femme et le development (ANFD), informed us of such issues in the Democratic Republic of Congo, *"where [an estimated] 90 per cent of youth are unemployed. Those who are employed are found in urban centres. While all young people living in rural areas are losing out [...] [inequalities exist:] a) Girls and boys have the same opportunity to study, [but] if their parents have little money, [...] they only send boys to study, and leave the girls [out]. b) The indigenous peasants form a group excluded from development activities. Finally, young people incur serious barriers to participation in work."*

- In addition, several participants believed that access to government jobs is largely based on nepotism and contacts, i.e. jobs are often given to people who know someone already working in a given department. Some participants also observed that these jobs are further often assigned to people from the governing political party.

Some country examples:

- The private sector in France was cited as permissive of discriminatory recruitment practices by requesting candidates to include a photo of themselves in their CVs.

- Yanira, 29, from Mexico told us, *"I started at the lowest position in a government department, but I gained respect as they saw my ability, honesty and commitment to work together [...] the most important thing is to not give up and learn new things every day."*

- In Peru, Maclovio, 27, with the "Organización, Asociación Educativa Ñam Sumi Perú" posted: *"I was at a workshop and at that time I was doing work with indigenous university students, one day I was extremely disappointed to hear and see that in my country there are still vestiges of hatred, and discrimination [...] the opinions expressed by so many young professionals against Indians was shocking: telling them 'to return to their village, because they are ignorant'. This social selfishness [...] prevails in our environment [...] and is why there is a divide between public and private universities. Universities should espouse social development, inclusion and equality, if we want to see it in our society."*

FINAL INSIGHTS

According to the United Nations Human Settlements Programme's (UN- HABITAT) 2009 Urban Youth Survey,[11] cities offer young people with higher levels of education greater opportunities to integrate into urban life than they do for the less educated. These findings point to education, especially for females, as a key driver in accessing the opportunities that come with urban life and taking advantage of them. Do you agree with this?

Participants from India, Kenya and Botswana all agreed. Kirthi, 24, from India told us: *"I think this statement is considerably true in India. Young people who have higher education on their side have a greater shot at landing jobs that let them be a part of urban life."*

Participants further commented that employment-related resources and services for young people are often not available in rural areas. Where they are offered, a lack of awareness or information may prevent rural youth from benefitting from them.

On disability and the role of information and communication technologies (ICTs), Awa, 30, with Impact Creators in Cameroon, commented:

"Youth civil society leaders, the physically challenged [and others] all have to participate and develop gender-friendly legal frameworks, and then propose them to their home governments and multilateral and bilateral organizations. The creation of multimedia [information and communication technology] ICT centres in rural areas will tremendously increase access to information for both male and female as well as physically challenged youths. We cannot undervalue the prowess of social networking sites nowadays as a tool for mobilization, citizenship and activism (political, social, etc.)."

[11] United Nations, Human Settlements Programme, 2010

Vote Corner:

What are your top 1-3 recommendations for policymakers towards ensuring young people are adequately and appropriately prepared for the job market?

The top three recommendations as voted by participants on the International Year of the Youth Facebook page were:

1) Provide practical opportunities and encourage entrepreneurship and alternative careers (72 per cent of votes);

2) After policies are put in place, ensure that they are enforced and implemented (17 per cent of votes);

3) Ensure practices in the work place are inclusive, non-discriminatory and promote equal opportunities (11 per cent of votes).

In addition to the above, several other recommendations were proposed. Most notably:

The majority agreed there is a need to improve the quality of education and to make it accessible to all young people. This requires tailoring curricula more effectively to the labour market, including through the development of practical skills (proposed by Muhamad, 20, with the Asian Law Students Association).

Mechanisms should be put in place by governments in partnership with the private sector; so that institutions are supporting internships and vocational training at scale and in a broad range of disciplines.

Vocational training, apprenticeships and non-formal education should be more widely recognized by employers as valuable components of a rounded education, which in turn would increase candidates' employment credentials and contribute towards a more stable labour market.

All governments should provide spaces for young people to share their views and discuss the issues they face with regard to education and employment (Yasmyn, 24, from Guadeloupe).

Governments and the private sector should ensure that information is widely available to all segments of the youth population and support those social groups which experience the most difficulties in accessing and completing education, such as young people living in extreme poverty and in rural locations, young women and youth with disabilities.

Yanira, 29, from Mexico suggested the following: "1) I recommend that before graduating from university, the government should assist with internship programmes at prestigious companies, whereby youth can acquire responsibilities and increase their competitive qualities. 2) According to the labour market, the government should create a fund to train young leaders in all of the main national educational institutions. They would promote the scheme internationally as well. 3) Design a strategy between governments and students, in which young people demonstrate their capabilities through community service, applying their knowledge in other countries, and empowering them to develop their team skills – preparing them for a working life."

FINAL INSIGHTS

Jelena, a participant at the X Central European Initiative Youth Forum, held in November 2010 (in Montenegro), informed us of the Forum's recommendations relating to education and employment of young people: *"The recommendations are based on the needs, experiences and good practices of Central European countries that were represented at the Forum."*

The outcome recommendations focus on "Strengthening instruments and programmes for the successful entry of youth into the labour market" and include (X Central European Initiative, 2010):

- Provide entrepreneurship learning in schools
- Provide opportunities for young people starting a business (loans, training, subsidies)
- Provide extensive and continuous analysis of market needs
- Provide education and training programmes that are tailored to market needs
- Provide social and economic integration of early school leavers/drop-outs
- Strengthen and promote the use of information centres and career counselling
- Promote volunteering as an excellent way of gaining knowledge, skills and competencies, and incentives for professional mobility
- Provide recognition and quality assurance in education and training
- Raise awareness of employers about the importance of non-formal education
- Increase visibility of youth in communities, promote and encourage the proactive role of youth

In addition to the Youth Forum above, the International Trade Union Confederation in Berlin organized an open space forum, entitled "Decent work for youth - lost in globalization?" in October 2011. More than 80 young people from 25 countries took part. Ivan, 26, with the Youth Section of the Union of Autonomous Trade Unions of Croatia, informed us that:

"Upon completion of the international conference, participants signed an open letter, called 'Young trade unionists call for action on youth employment at the International Labour Conference 2012,' which will be referred to the International Labour Organization, the International Trade Union Confederation and other trade union organizations around the world."

CHAPTER CONCLUSIONS

With regard to youth transitions from education into the work place, some key themes emerged from week II. These were:

Many higher education systems and institutions around the world are still insufficiently tailored and aligned to the practical and dynamic needs of the labour market. As Ivan, 26, from Croatia eloquently stated, *"academic institutions are focused too much on theoretical learning, and not enough on practical skills."* All types of higher education, including formal, non-formal and informal are essential tools for young people to succeed in the labour market.

Developing leadership qualities among diverse youth is vital if innovative solutions to job scarcity are to be found at scale. Not only are such qualities (often associated with life skills, such as problem-solving and critical and creative thinking) empowering on a personal level, but they are also coping mechanisms for young people during difficult economic, social and political times. Hikmat, 21, from Afghanistan reflected:

"I believe that passion and commitment is the key for a strong leader to do what's right and the best for their country folk or followers. In my opinion, a great leader doesn't need to be reminded of what to do, instead [s/]he shows excellence in what [s/]he does, such that [s/]he walks what [s/]he talks."

Encouraging the capacity of youth to be proactive is vital during challenging times. Hira, 23, from Pakistan (studying in the United States) urged fellow participants to:

"Check the websites of country offices of large international organizations in your own country, it always helps. Talk to people and be very proactive. That's my advice for all the young people! At this age, we expect that everything would come to us easily, but no one gets it until they put in an effort!"

Internships and volunteering can offer young people opportunities to develop their life skills and help increase their chances of finding a job. Furthermore they may even contribute towards youth supporting peer learning, such as young entrepreneurs like Janine, from South Africa, who told us:

"I am working on a concept that is looking to place young college and university grad[uate]s in projects that give them real experience. Not internships where they get coffee and update lists. There are internship opportunities available, but they are heavily centred around the areas of engineering, [information technology] IT, finance and law. I want to begin with the areas of grad[uate]s from the marketing, communications and digital sectors. I also want to start a platform for volunteering for youth, an area with tremendous opportunities."

For more comments on entrepreneurship, see chapter IV.

But the question remains [...] how can we meet the aspirations of young people? An e4e - Education for Employment: Realizing Arab Youth Potential video clip suggests some of the linkages between education and future employment. Steffi, 29, remarked on the e-discussion platform after watching the clip that:

"The e4e education for employment initiative could not have come at a better time, as it addresses problems that go beyond the Arab World. Youth unemployment remains one of the biggest challenges in the Asia-Pacific region, where youth account for half of the region's jobless - and the skills mismatch being one part of the problem. I agree that the solution must come from a united effort among governments, the private sector and educational institutions, but also, importantly, the trade unions and civil society actors to make sure that the rights of young workers to decent work are always part of the mix. In some cases (especially in the developed world), we have witnessed an increase in precarious employment for young people, who have often little choice but to accept whatever job they can get, so a crucial question remains - how can we not only create skills that match the labour market, but also quality jobs that match the aspirations of young people?"

Indeed, this was one of the questions debated by organizations and Heads of State at the Building Future Education MENA [Middle East and North Africa] events in October 2011. The private sector certainly has a stronger role to play with regard to improving education and increasing the employment opportunities for the youth of today.

Loubna, 23-year-old woman from Morocco

I am a 23-year-old female student from Morocco, majoring in finance with a minor in international studies. As required by my international studies programme, I undertook my first volunteer position for a period of one month in 2007 with a Moroccan youth-focused non-governmental organization (NGO). Later, I volunteered with several education-focused NGOs, until I started to work with an organization that deals with women's rights and family affairs, called Fédération de la ligue démocratique pour les droits de la femme (FLDDF). My hard work resulted in being elected — as the first young woman under 22 — to the Fédération's Board of Directors. What is more, I was responsible for the Fédération's youth branch, whose main activities involved educating young people about current life issues and engaging them in civic life.

Through my academic programme, I participated in national and international conferences about cultural exchange, politics and the environment, and have come to understand that today's major world issue is the environment and sustainability. In fact, the climate in Morocco is changing for the worse and is having a negative impact on the country's agriculture. This year, I participated in the Rio+20 preparations by working on influencing the outcome of the United Nations Conference on Sustainable Development (Rio+20) on behalf of Moroccan youth in order to reflect their perspective on environmental changes and the action that they can take in their communities regarding sustainable development.

My involvement with Rio+20 led me to work with the Earth Charter, where, in October 2011, I was appointed as Country Activator Focal Point in Morocco. This position has given me the opportunity to enlarge my network in the sustainability field in order to collaborate with other Country Activator Focal Points, mainly in Africa. I am now even more involved in environmental issues and am trying to link these with issues of unemployment, gender and education, focusing on rural areas where agriculture is the main source of livelihood and on green jobs. I am looking forward to making my community more aware about our environment, as it is our Earth that we live in and that will be for us and for future youth.

I am currently seeking to be a focal point on climate change for North Africa within YOUNGO (the constituency of youth NGOs participating in United Nations climate change negotiations) for the next Conference of the Parties (COP) conference. My volunteer work is providing valuable experience needed to achieve my related career goals. Volunteering with organizations helps to develop practical skills that are needed in the labour market. It also helps to learn more about today's issues and how they are related to one's own community, as well as to build strong networks with youth from around the world, so that knowledge and experience is shared.

Yasmyn, 24-year-old woman from Guadeloupe

Born and raised in Guadeloupe (a French island in the Caribbean), the "butterfly island", I left for Paris at age 18 to pursue my dental medicine studies. Yet I soon discovered that this field was not personally fulfilling, Instead, I decided to switch to a bachelor's programme in biology, ecology and evolution. Following a deep desire to broaden my horizons and further travel, I applied to an environmental science master's degree programme in Montreal, Canada. A few months later, I settled in Montreal, a small, peaceful and stress-free city that I love!

FINDING AN INTERNSHIP: BELIEVE IN YOURSELF AS STRONGLY AS YOU EVER HAVE!

In October 2011, the time arrived for students to find an internship. My interest was in the national and international environmental institutions located in Montreal. What does finding an internship entail? Is it convincing a recruiter that you are the student s/he is looking for? But how? By drawing on your professional experiences, regardless of their number; your personality traits, such as flexibility, efficiency, productivity, versatility and creativity; and your skills. This seemed very difficult for me, as I had been in the environmental field for just under two years, and had had only one internship experience.

Another problem I had to confront was that, here in Canada, foreign students are in competition with Canadian citizens. Even if you have the best profile, your immigration status might lose you a job to a citizen.

Compared to other students, I was feeling underqualified and inadequate. I did not know how to persuade recruiters to choose me and to trust in me if I did not do so myself.

Two interviews later, I had still not found an internship. As I pondered the situation, buoyed by chocolate, I realized that, in fact, fear was holding me back from achieving my personal goals. In early December 2011, when I was interviewed for the third time, I decided to remain relaxed, and to put the immigration issue out of my mind.

A couple of weeks later, I was pleasantly surprised to learn that the Ministry of Environment of Quebec selected me as the new intern for its Environmental Evaluation Department's office for renewable energy.

This experience has taught me that you have to believe strongly in yourself and remain persistent in the face of barriers. When you equip yourself with the right tools, you can achieve your dreams and succeed in life. Fear only makes us weaker, so never give up hope. And above all, love yourself and stay positive!

Additional resources

International Labour Organization (2008). Apprenticeships in the informal economy in Africa. Workshop report, Geneva, 3-4 May 2007. Employment Sector: Employment Report, No. 1. Geneva: International Labour Office. Available from http://www.ilo.org/public/english/employment/download/report/report1.pdf

Morrison, Andrew, and Shwetlena Sabarwal (2008). The economic participation of adolescent girls and young women: why does it matter? PREMnotes Gender, No. 128 (December). Washington, D.C.: World Bank. Available from http://siteresources.worldbank.org/INTGENDER/Resources/morrison_sabarwal08.pdf

United Nations Development Group-Millennium Development Goals Network (2011). Report of the e-discussion on education: closing the gap, held from 1 February to 4 March 2011 as part of preparation for the United Nations Economic and Social Council's 2011 Annual Ministerial Review on education.

United Nations, Entity for Gender Equality and the Empowerment of Women (2010). Report on the online discussion on gender, education and employment, 7-20 July 2010. Unpublished paper. Available from http://www.un.org/womenwatch/daw/csw/csw55/onlinediscussion3.html

Young Workers' Blog (2011). Available from http://www.itfglobal.org/youngworkersblog/

Youth Employment Network (2007). The time for youth is now. Youth Employment Network Brochure. Available from http://www.ilo.org/public/english/employment/yen/downloads/brochure/brochure.pdf

"Youth are a **vast resource** but are often treated as a constituency that needs to be managed, instead of engaged and supported to play an **influential role** in their respective countries to develop the globe." – Akampa

UN Photo/Martine Perret
January 2010 | Timor-Leste

CHAPTER III
LOOKING FOR A JOB

AN EMERGING PICTURE: THE INCREASING LENGTH OF YOUTH JOB SEARCHES

Recent statistics on youth employment present a gloomy state of affairs for today's young people. In most developed economies, the long-term unemployment rates of youth significantly surpass those of adults. For example, in Italy, the gap between the youth and adult long-term unemployment rates is shocking: youth are three times more likely than adults to be unemployed for at least one year.[1]

Of particular concern is the increasing length of job searches, which is not only leading to severe frustration and the disillusionment of young people, but also to increasing numbers falling out of the labour force entirely. The International Labour Organization recently reported that:

"In 56 countries for which comparable monthly/quarterly data were available, the youth labour force expanded by far less during the crisis than would be expected: [...] there were 2.6 million fewer youth in the labour market in 2010 than expected based on longer-term (pre-crisis) trends".[2]

These are precarious times for many young people across the globe. However, within this uncertain climate, there is growing political will to address youth development issues. Since the Africa Commission's seminal report,[3] there has been increasing momentum in Africa to respond to alarming statistics: that globally, "by 2025, one out of every four young people under 25 will be from Africa".[4] This population explosion will have a dramatic knock-on effect on the labour market, where "there is a[n urgent] need to create 10 to 15 million jobs a year to absorb the huge number of young people becoming part of the African labour force".[5]

Hence, since 2009, there have been several high-level policy forums that aim to tackle the growing "youth bulges" and soaring rates of youth unemployment. The High-Level Meeting of the General Assembly on Youth in 2011 emphasized the importance of youth employment, calling for targeted and integrated national youth employment policies for inclusive job creation, skills development and vocational training to meet specific labour market demands. At the 17th Ordinary African Union (AU) Summit, which was held in June-July 2011 under the theme, Accelerating Youth Empowerment for Sustainable Development, the United Nations Deputy Secretary-General, Asha-Rose Migiro, reminded Heads of State of the possibility of growing conflict associated with high youth unemployment and high population growth rates:

[1] International Labour Organization, 2011b, pp. 2-3
[2] Globally, the youth labour force participation rate decreased from 49.4 per cent in 2009 to 48.8 per cent, with the largest regional decreases in the Developed Economies & European Union and South Asia (International Labour Organization, 2011b, p. 2).
[3] Realizing the Potential of Africa's Youth (2009)
[4] Secretariat of the Africa Commission, 2009, p.12
[5] ibid.

"If we are to bring lasting peace and sustainable development to the continent, we must empower Africa's youth [...] For too many young adults in Africa, this is a time of dashed hopes, frustration, and political, economic and social exclusion," said Ms. Migiro. "But there is a way for African nations to defuse the youth time bomb – by empowering youth and reaping the benefits".[6]

At the national level, there are many complex challenges for young job seekers, which sadly often relate to socio-political factors and deep-seated exclusionary policies and practices. In January 2011, the South African Institute of Race Relations found that 51 per cent of young people between 15 and 24 are unemployed. But this statistic only scratches the surface: among those unemployed youth in South Africa, 63 per cent are young African (black South African) women, whereas this figure is only 15 per cent for young Indian (Indian South African) men. Furthermore, the youth unemployment rate varies considerably between races - it is 57 per cent among young Africans (black South Africans), 23 per cent among young Indians (Indian South Africans), and 21 per cent among young whites (white South Africans).[7]

This paints a disturbing picture of social inequality, not only in terms of access to decent work and job-seeking services, but also retention. While this is a particularly acute problem in South Africa, young job seekers across the globe are still excluded from the labour force based on gender, ethnicity, ability/disability and geography. Some of the participants on the e-discussion platform mentioned briefly some of these issues. However, it remains a sensitive area. How can these gross inequalities remain and still be prevalent in the year 2011?

STILL SEARCHING: A GLOBALIZED WORLD DOES NOT NECESSARILY MEAN MORE OPPORTUNITIES FOR GROWTH

During the week of 25 to 31 October, week III, the e-discussion platform was open to all to discuss the topic of "looking for a job." The e-discussion invited the views of young people aged 15 to 30,[8] as well as representatives of youth-led organizations. More than 310 comments were posted on the e-discussion platform by young women and men aged 16 to 30 from all corners of the world, including Nigeria, Bangladesh, the United Kingdom and the Bolivarian Republic of Venezuela. In addition to the e- discussion site, there were also postings and uploads onto the United Nations International Year of Youth Facebook page, and a live question and answer Twitter session with United Nations Youth Champion Monique Coleman.

The views conveyed throughout this chapter focus on young people's entry into the labour market. Almost all of the participants shared both positive and negative experiences of job searching. Indeed, there was no overall consensus as to whether globalization (as represented by such factors as use of information and communication technologies (ICTs) or working abroad, etc.) is,

[6] United Nations, Department of Public Information, 2011
[7] South African Institute of Race Relations, 2011
[8] This is taking into account both the United Nations definition of youth (15- to 24-year-olds) and many local cultural contexts and understandings.

in general, favourable or not. What was made clear was that many educated young people around the globe are, as recently stated by the International Labour Organization, in "working poverty." Whereas the technical definition of being in "working poverty" is working while in a family household that lives below the poverty line (US$1.25 a day per person), several of the participants viewed it in a broader sense: as being underemployed and/or in jobs that they don't see as having long-term prospects. Jimmy from Zambia, for example, replied that his understanding of working poverty relates to:

"...an increase in corruption and nepotism. As a result, youths cannot get jobs easily, especially through the formal channels. Youth are therefore facing working poverty because they are involved in jobs which are not in line with what they are qualified for. In addition, they are often exploited through internships which are not well remunerated."

Despite this, many of the participants remained hopeful. As Nduta, a student at the University of KwaZulu-Natal in Durban, South Africa, exclaimed: the secret to getting that dream job is to *"start small and grow, learn and acquire skills as you progress."* We now turn to some of the most perceptive comments shared:

WHAT YOUNG PEOPLE SAY

In your country, what kinds of job guidance initiatives (organizations and resources) exist?

The main initiatives reported by participants included:

- Business and social networks (both informal and formal).

- Youth-focused organizations. For example, Solomon from Ghana, who works with Global Youth Innovation Network (GYIN), explained how GYIN has created an online network where youth can meet and share knowledge and experiences. For him, this has meant, *"as an entrepreneur managing a startup company, providing professional [information technology] IT services to farmers in Ghana, [and] the business networks have been most beneficial."*

- Career fairs or annual graduate recruitment programmes – especially at universities and colleges. Career fairs seem to be taking place at many universities, as mentioned by Preneshni, 22, a South African student. However, she also pointed out that *"there is often a small spectrum of businesses coming to these fairs, something that might only make them relevant to a limited number of students."*

- Internships - which were found to assist young people with decision-making on career paths. Inger (in her mid 20s) from South Africa recommended making work experience compulsory for high school students, in order to help them choose the right career path.

- Assistance with CV/resumé and cover letter writing, and use of social media tools. An example of the provision of these was online recruitment agencies, which helped Germaine, a female in her mid-20s from South Africa, to get a job.

- Finally, Mitch (a young lecturer at the University of KwaZulu-Natal, South Africa) suggested that, *"it is not the responsibility of educational institutions to train students in job hunting,"* rather these institutions should facilitate the development of skills that are more suited for job hunting so that quality education provides a solid foundation for the transition from academic work into a job. This was certainly thought-provoking!

Tweet Corner

Some of the tweets from week III

RT @UNpYouth: [networking skills can be useful...how you interact/relate w/ people can be the advantage that sets you apart]#youthjobs
http://t.co/TFea94Ow

RT @UNpYouth: [You r always asked to have 2-4 years work experience, where r young ppl supp. 2 get this experience from?]
http://t.co/TFea94Ow#youthjobs

In your experience, what have you used and what was the most helpful?

- Several of the participants from both the Asian and African regions found that business and social networks (informal and formal) were the most useful source of career guidance. This included membership in youth networks which use online resources, such as Globcal, Connect African Development and opportunitiesforyouth.org.

- In general, participants were positive about using social media in job searches, but a few also mentioned that there were challenges to be overcome; namely, not having the desired qualifications. Hikmat, 21, from Afghanistan and a member of Peshawar Youth Organization explained his experiences: *"social media helped me access new jobs, although I was not eligible for any of them because of the request for work experience and a Master's Degree."* Similarly, Seabe, 23, from Botswana confirmed this: *"apart from internships, fresh graduates are finding it difficult to find employment. This is because often companies advertise job positions for candidates with 3 years [experience] and above."*

● Most participants also spoke about internships (paid or unpaid) as being a very useful form of job guidance. Ayshah, 26, from Kenya shared her experience: *"...when [I] was an intern I used that opportunity to expand my network and [...] market myself, especially when I was told to represent the organization in general – and it helped a lot, because by the end of the internship I left a legacy!"*

● Finally, many of our young participants mentioned that the most helpful approach for job searching is to maintain a positive outlook, including self-motivation and perseverance. Inger (a Swede studying in South Africa) explained how a combination of social networks and personal resources helped her secure her current job: *"I am a strong believer in social networking, and I think it can be very effective in learning more about employment opportunities that exist. I got my current job after debating with my now boss in a Master's class!"*

How did you access / secure your first job?

● The e-discussion revealed that it took participants varying lengths of time to get their first job. It took Nduta, a student at KwaZulu-Natal University (originally from Kenya), seven years to get a stable paying job after high school. During those seven years, she volunteered for an organization that works with vulnerable children in Nairobi's slums. This experience taught her not to give up.

● Volunteerism and internships emerged as important approaches to securing a first job, by enabling individuals to gain experience and develop networks. Fortune from Nigeria shared her path; she started as a trainee in an information and communication technology (ICT) training and education centre and worked her way up from there. Now, after several years of work experience, she is about to begin a Master of Science degree programme. Fortune's advice: *"the work you do for free today will equip you for the income you will earn tomorrow."*

● Respondents emphasized that getting a job requires a lot of dedication and patience. Eva, 21, from Spain had just found a job and described how the combination of a good CV, promoting her blog, sending many applications and *"insisting and showing confidence"* finally secured her a job with a hotel chain.

Young job seekers shared that it was very important to have social networks, as these linked individuals with jobs as well as information-sharing. For Ayshah, 26, from Kenya, social networks were what enabled her to secure her first job as a promoter in a supermarket after she had *"applied everywhere"* without success. Fortune from Nigeria had a less positive experience. She explained how there are many barriers contributing to people's struggles with job searching: their level of education, the *"excessive obsession for qualifications and certifications"* and the fact that *"jobs tend to be restricted within informal social networks (familial and friendship ties)."* However, she reminds us:

"In as much as we look out for opportunities, we must also note that opportunities can be created; volunteering is one very useful way of creating opportunities for oneself. Opportunities exist even beyond the confines of a person's national borders. This is why the internet is very useful today. I cannot deny the fact that most of the opportunities that have come my way in terms of learning, networking and self-development are largely attributable to the internet and how I have explored it over the years (actively for about a decade now)."

Three Word Tag: Job Searching Guidance

Participants were also asked:

"from whom, what, and where have you received the best job searching guidance? For example: 'father; persistence; home.'" These were some of the responses received:

Participant	From Whom	From What	From Where
Luis, 24, Dominican Republic	father's friend	patience	office
Seabe, 23, Botswana	career advisors	persistence	university
Amadou, 24, Senegal	google	persistence	online
Alexander, 25, Mexico	professor	making proposals	university
Lara, 21, United Kingdom	father	ambition	university

Vote Corner:

What are your top 3 tips for other young job hunters?

After several suggestions were submitted to the e-discussion platform, participants voted on the most talked-about submissions via the Facebook page. The top three tips were:

1) Ambition: have a "can do" attitude, take action and make things happen. This tip received 66 per cent of the votes. This can be done through working on the way one presents oneself, or by using volunteering as a way to a more stable job or to starting one's own business. Sibeso, a 25-year-old female from Zambia working with the United Nations Youth Association of Zambia (YUNA ZAMBIA), wrote: "My fellow youths, I would advise you to start becoming your own bosses by starting up your own businesses, rather than waiting to get employed. Remember: we are not growing any younger – but older – by the day."

2) Perseverance: do not give up. This received 18 per cent of the votes. Tinghua stated: "Always look on the bright side of life: If you failed a job interview, at least you accumulated interview experience."

3) Social networks (formal or informal) – build and make use of these. This also received 18 per cent of the votes. Joe, 24, from the United Kingdom, who has never been unemployed, explained how he had spent months working to help his friends find jobs: by improving their CVs, giving interview advice and organizing interviews. Four of his friends have now secured jobs. He stated: "Your friends with jobs have knowledge about the process. Get that knowledge. If you have a job, share your knowledge with others."

OTHERS ON FACEBOOK MENTIONED THAT THEIR BEST JOB SEARCHING TIPS CAME FROM

- Peers (Ahmad)
- Self-motivation (Shivani)
- Drawing a map of core values and names of organizations (As well as signing up for newsletters and positive thinking) (Thanh)
- Personal effort (Nosakhare)
- Networking and knowing yourself (Amanda)

How does globalization have positive and/or negative effects on your – and your friends' – efforts to secure a job?

Globalization describes the processes by which economies, societies and cultures have become integrated through communication, transportation and technology. The participants on the e-discussion platform focused on the movement of young people across borders and increased access to new resources – including communication technology.

ON THE UPSIDE

- Mobility and removing barriers: Globalization processes have opened up opportunities for young people looking for jobs. For Karolina, 27, from Sweden (studying in South Africa), globalization – through the removal of economic barriers and the opening up of borders – has enabled her to move (unforced) from her country of origin to other countries (such as the United Kingdom and Norway) in search of work. Regional agreements which govern travel and conditions of employment have created opportunities at both the national and international levels.

- The same sentiments on the benefits of mobility from globalization are echoed by Ayshah, 26, from Kenya, who observes that the advent of globalization has spurred intra- and inter-country movement (which is not forced). She is originally from a central region of Kenya, but due to a lack of opportunities there, she has now settled in another Kenyan coastal region which generates wealth from foreign tourists, and where it was easier for her to secure employment.

- In Jordan, Enass, 25, tells us that globalization has resulted in new information technology (IT) and software companies being set up. *"Many international companies are investing in and opening new companies in this country – they look to outsource here because we have qualified people in this industry with lower labour costs than in Europe."* Furthermore, there has been a transfer of technology from one country to another, which can lead to innovative job creation.

- Eva, 21, from Spain (who works for a hotel chain) told us that: *"the ability to speak a diversity of languages can be both an opportunity and a challenge (as a result of globalization) for young people."*

ON THE DOWNSIDE

- Muhamad, 20, from Indonesia perceives globalization as having the potential to increase competition for already scarce jobs. He argues that globalization means that young people, who in most cases have little or no work experience, are made to compete for jobs with people with vast work experience. In this regard, it is the youth *"who suffer in the end"* as a result of globalization (particularly if they are exploited due to inexperience).

- In addition, Big, 24, from Zimbabwe believes that globalization is benefiting developed economies. He views this in light of *"brain drain,"* whereby improved transport and communication networks between countries have made it easier for developed economies to attract professionals from developing economies, thereby *"leaving behind people who do not have the necessary innovative and entrepreneurial skills"* to take developing countries forward.

- According to Jack, globalization has contributed to unemployment because of what he referred to as *"labour fragmentations."* In other words, globalization brings about the interconnectedness of economies, which has contributed to the current global economic crisis. Even the current crisis in the euro zone affects most other countries. In a sense, *"globalization spreads instability."*

FINAL INSIGHTS

Joseph from Latvia told us: *"The situation in Latvia is not good. We still have the third highest unemployment rate among [European Union] EU members. While Leo from Spain shared his opinion about emigration as the only solution, about 15 per cent of Latvian citizens have moved to another country, like Germany, Scandinavian countries, Ireland and the [United Kingdom] UK. I love my country, but I'm concerned about staying here [...] As a result of this huge emigration wave from Latvia, those who are left here in the near future will have to pay huge taxes to support the social insurance system, and that will cause another problem – a shadow economy."*

What do you think will be the biggest opportunities and challenges faced by young job seekers in the future?

OPPORTUNITIES

- Muhamad, 20, from Indonesia saw a bright future for youth around the globe. He told us that there will be more new opportunities for young people which do not currently exist. However, he also views the increased competition in *"this era of globalization, which makes us compete with other youth in the world,"* as a challenge, but one which will ensure that young people will therefore seek to improve their skills in order to be competitive in the job market.

● Seabe, 23, from Botswana told us that, *"there are many African entrepreneurs; young, energetic and optimistic. I have a couple of friends who have started small businesses, mostly in the [information and communication technology] ICT sector, and some of them are actually competing with big brand names."* Instead of waiting for that dream job, Seabe encourages all to be proactive and industrious!

● According to Dulal, with the National Federation of Youth Organizations in Bangladesh, that federation ran a programme which targeted *"480 rural poor youths, who received training on livestock and poultry farming. A revolving fund was then setup to provide loans to the trained youths to establish income-generating businesses."* The federation thus seeks to develop entrepreneurial skills in these young people. This for Dulal is a window of future opportunities and possibilities in Bangladesh.

● Michael, 23, from Italy and the World Esperanto Youth Organization, saw a future in the green economy:

"As young people tend to be more interested in trying out new ideas and developing new solutions, I think that they are more likely to be employed in fields connected with new, green technologies. Furthermore, young people are, in general, more conscious of global issues like climate change and social equity. For this reason, I think that promotion of green economies among youth is a winning solution [...]"

For more information on green jobs, see chapter IV.

CHALLENGES

● In Botswana, Seabe, 23, informed us that graduates spend a lot of time looking for employment – in fact, *"between two and five years."* According to him, the government and other organizations in Botswana cannot cope with the increasing number of graduates. (A similar sentiment was expressed by Enass, 25, from Jordan.) Seabe goes on to say that efforts to create employment in the form of internships have further worsened the difficulties of these young job seekers, who are now *"being exploited and in most cases are expected to undertake unmatched jobs."* Another challenge is the significant amount of work experience that is required by several organizations, whereas young graduates often do not have any work-related experience. Finally, he argues that the government needs to be more creative in exploring possible new areas/sectors for employment, rather than focusing solely on farming and other agricultural areas.

- Yasmyn, 24, from Guadeloupe reflected that most people who are affected by unemployment in her country are those who do not have the necessary qualifications (such as diplomas). She also highlights racial discrimination as another persistent obstacle for many to attain meaningful employment in Guadeloupe.

- Lara, 21, a law student from the United Kingdom (UK), saw the application process to practice as a lawyer in the UK as a major obstacle in searching for and securing future employment. *"It is often a four-stage process, and while doing a degree at the same time can be extremely difficult."*

- Bijay, 27, with the Association of Youth Organizations in Nepal, told us about the challenges he sees both present and in the foreseeable future:

"Working as part of civil society or as an [non-governmental organization] NGO is sometimes difficult, particularly in dealing with political parties. There is a triangular situation: on one side there is the NGO, at another corner are the political parties, and thirdly there is the government. A kind of opposing culture is developing. They are always complaining that NGOs are not working properly. There is also age-based discrimination. Being a youth, it is sometimes difficult to work. Thus, a good platform for youth should be created. Even NGOs and [international NGOs] INGOs are creating youth panels [and] volunteer groups; but even here, youth are being used for their own causes. Youth [are still restricted] and can't make a meaningful contribution towards policy or programmes. If youth are [not] supported to develop their knowledge, then conflict can take place."

If you are currently employed – is your job secure? Do you have several part-time jobs? Do you have benefits, such as insurance? Are you making use of your skills and qualifications? If not, is this your choice or due to underemployment?

Participants on the e-discussion platform during week III included a trainee lawyer, a member of a biodiversity-focused non-governmental organization, a social media officer and an amateur writer (of poetry and novels).

The following were the main issues discussed:

- The majority of participants were either unemployed, still completing their education, doing unpaid or part-time work, completing short-term contracts or "small jobs," or engaged in several of these activities at one time. For example, Alejandro, 25, from Mexico works as a university teacher and is guaranteed a certain number of hours per week, which conforms with all Mexican labour laws. He is using this opportunity to get his Master's degree to help further his goal – which is to work in the Mexican Foreign Service.

- Many participants indicated that they did lack job benefits, such as insurance, and experience underemployment, holding jobs that did not match their qualifications. Hamadullah, 24, from Pakistan told us that he is employed but his job is insecure, because he *"may be called off anytime."* In addition, he believes that he is not making full use of his skills and qualifications, and that most young people in Pakistan work without signing any contract with their employers!

- Due to unemployment and lack of work experience, some young people are either participating in internship programmes or are volunteering.

- There was a general consensus that, through ambition, perseverance and gaining experience, one's true career path will eventually be recognized later in life.

Poem Corner

Looking for a Job | Terna, Nigeria

LOOKING FOR A JOB

I have heard that name echo nearby,
Or should I swear its shadow went by;
Not now, feels nothing like a day-dream,
Gave many years of my life.
To work a job, and feel alive,
It is there in my nightly dream,
I created it doubly in my imagination.
Perfect, with no trace of illusion,
Still I await its long coming;
Will cheer it like a lost son's homecoming.
I have walked many a town side street,
Tired, wet and hot from heat;
From sunrise to sunset to woo a job,
Mail me the opening for that job!

(http://www.facebook.com/UNyouthyear/posts/10150893186455290)

If you are employed, are you in your ideal job?
If not, how are you trying to reach your goal?

- The majority of young participants informed us that they have not yet secured their ideal job, largely due to a lack of work experience. Several young people would ideally like to work in business, diplomacy, human rights and computer science/ technology.

- Jimmy, 26, from Zambia reminded us of the importance of volunteering. He volunteers at the United Nations Youth Association of Zambia, and decided to volunteer because he could not secure his ideal job. His frustrations continue, however, as there is still a mismatch between his qualifications and the voluntary role he is performing.

- Amadou, 24, from Senegal also highlighted the importance of work-related internships, as they allow individuals *"to utilize their skills and knowledge, and at the same time build on their work experience."*

- Some positive comments came from Fortunate, a young African, who stated that she is engaged in her ideal job as a project officer. However, she advises other young job seekers that in order to get their ideal jobs, *"they need to develop their social networking skills, as this can expand opportunities for employment."*

Have you managed to create an opportunity out of a crisis?
Are there any Middle Eastern entrepreneurs out there?
Are there any African Mark Zuckerburgs?
Or Asian philanthropists?

Seabe, 23, from Botswana recalled a chance encounter that he had earlier this year on a bus with an elderly person who said, "young people of this generation are well equipped, with technology, an inquisitive mind, schools to attend, programmes to follow, and at times people to guide you in your endeavours."

He went on to say that, "young people have nothing to lose in becoming entrepreneurs and hence we shouldn't be afraid to reach out for our dreams and take risks." Seabe told us this had an impact on him: "I took his advice and I have been pitching ideas to a few investors for small start-ups." So – let's see what happens for Seabe!

How can we hold policymakers and governments to account for ensuring youth unemployment rates are reduced?

Responses included:

- Amadou, 24, from Senegal said, *"there is a need to lobby governments so that the issue is included in government planning."* This call to activism and direct action was also agreed upon by Seabe, 23, from Botswana, Aku, 30, from Togo, and Lara, 21, from the United Kingdom. Lara reminded us that:

  "Youth unemployment is a serious problem for the future of the economy and mindset of a generation, and policymakers need to be constantly aware of this. So, pressure groups and surveys being done to collate evidence and put pressure on governments to make change would be an efficient way to hold policymakers to account."

- Ayshah, 26, from Kenya told us that governments should promote the creation of *"job opportunities for young people by funding and developing informal training and volunteering opportunities."*

- Yasmyn, 24, from Guadeloupe also agreed that governments should be encouraged to promote and develop flexible jobs for young people.

Twitterview

With Monique Coleman, United Nations Youth Champion

United Nations Youth Champion, Monique Coleman (@gimmemotalk), was hosted by the United Nations Focal Point on Youth for a one-hour Twitter interview on: twitter.com/UNpYouth. Youth from around the world posed questions to Monique about various youth employment issues, including her own experiences and advice. Monique provided a down-to-earth perspective of her working life, even sharing her first job – babysitting! Some of Monique's most notable quotes included:

"Sometimes people don't see opportunities in front of them because they are clouded by a lack of belief in themselves."

"Remember that you are not alone. So, find other people who are in similar situations & see how you can combine talents."

"I strongly encourage entrepreneurship! Also social business. @Yunus_Centre has a great model for social business."

Some of the notable comments sent to Monique by young people included:

"The foundation of every State is the education and awareness of its youth. without that #youthjobs seem unreal."

"What about #green #youthjobs and making this a priority for #rioplus20 #EarthSummit?"

"More #youthjobs can be created by skill development on indigenous knowledge and modern technical skills."

CHAPTER CONCLUSIONS

Some key themes that emerged from week III's discussion on looking for jobs were:

The experiences of several participants illustrated what recent research has shown: that more young people around the world are in a situation of working poverty, rather than are out of a job and looking for work. However, the majority of participants on the e-discussion platform understood "working poverty" in a broader sense (than the International Labour Organization definition). For young people such as Jimmy from Zimbabwe, for example, *"Youth are [...] facing working poverty because they are involved in jobs which are not in line with what they are qualified for."*

Indeed, a thoughtful comment regarding the pressures of being "a youth" was posted by Akampa: *"Youth are a vast resource but are often treated as a constituency that needs to be managed, instead of engaged and supported to play an influential role in their respective countries to develop the globe."* This theme of youth as potential threats will be picked up in the following chapter.

In order to tackle the pressures of unemployment and lack of work experience, many young people, such as Ayshah, 26, from Kenya and Fortune from Nigeria, are seeking internship or volunteering opportunities in order to develop their workplace skills. This echoes the voices we heard during week II on the platform. It also suggests that, not only are internships and volunteering opportunities being used as part of a young person's educational development, but also as a mechanism for direct job searching and networking.

There was however, no overall consensus as to whether globalization (as represented by such factors as use of information and communication technologies (ICTs) or working abroad, etc.) is, in general, positive or negative. However, there was a general consensus that through ambition, perseverance and gaining experience, many youth will eventually reach their career aspirations. Farhana, with Relations in Motion in Bangladesh, posted this inspirational comment on the International Year of Youth Facebook page:

"Let's change the world by innovative ideas along with YOUTH POWER. Focus on Quality, not quantity. Think of Construction, not destruction. Work with Motivation, not depression. Search Originality, not piracy. Unite for Unity, not partiality. Finally, go for Creativity and remove disparity. That's our Motto. Join us and develop YOURSELF."

CASE STUDY
Enass, 25-year-old woman from Jordan

In 2008, I graduated with a Bachelor of Science degree in information technology (IT), and now I work in the IT and software development industry. I think globalization has had a great positive effect on my employment and hiring experience, because there are many international companies and investors opening new businesses and investing in – as well as outsourcing to – Jordan, particularly in this field. Jordan has a highly-skilled population and lower labour costs than Europe and many other areas, which provide for a huge number of jobs for local workers and recent graduates like me. Jordanians are very proud that their country has been called the Silicon Valley of the Middle East. In light of this, since my university days, I prepared myself very well for the job market. I took many relevant courses and obtained certificates, and also got technical experience by serving as an intern and trainee in three companies while in university.

When graduation approached, I prepared a long list of all IT companies I had ever heard about, compiling their websites and contact information. I also prepared my CV and sought advice on it from some employed friends. Then I sent my CV to all of the company e-mail addresses on my list. Without the internet and other information and communication technologies, I would not have been able to learn about many of the companies in my field, or to prepare a strong CV and share it with those companies. In less than one month, while still in the final exam period of my last semester, I got two interviews and received my first job offer to be a software developer. Less than one month after that, following graduation, I got many other interviews and better offers, so I accepted my first official job contract with another company.

Two years later, although I was satisfied with my current employer, I wanted to develop new experience and so began to apply for jobs in different companies. After a few months of interviews and scanning offers, I got my second job with a bank in Switzerland, working in its offshore office in Jordan and also outsourcing with another European company. Over more than one and a half years, I gained important software development experience in that company. Currently, however, I am working for my third employer, doing the same job in the same field, but with an Emirati investor who has a company in the United Arab Emirates but who is investing in Jordan because of its high-calibre work force.

Based on my personal experience, I can say that there are a lot of opportunities available in my country, especially in the IT sector, with many start-up enterprises and significant external investment. Yet new graduates need to be aware of what companies are looking for, because there is a lot of competition out there. Young workers should distinguish themselves to employers by developing good distinctive competencies, being knowledgeable about their candidacy, and being able to prove themselves. Of course, that is not an easy task! But it is definitely doable.

Additional resources

International Labour Organization, Youth Employment Programme (YEP). Information available from http://www.ilo.org/employment/areas/youth-employment/lang--en/index.htm

International Labour Organization and United Nations Department of Economic and Social Affairs. Fact sheet on youth employment. Available from http://social.un.org/youthyear/docs/youth-employment.pdf

Ramdoss, Santhosh, Ashleigh Mullinax and Lara Storm (2011). Financial inclusion of youth – reaching the next generation. Screencast of presentation to the United States Agency for International Development Microenterprise Development Office's After Hours Seminar, No. 55. Washington, D.C., 1 September. Available from http://microlinks.kdid.org/library/financial-inclusion-youth-reaching-next-generation-presentation-and-screencast

Columbia University, School of International and Public Affairs (2008). Market Assessment Toolkit for Vocational Training Providers and Youth: linking vocational training programmes to market opportunities. New York: Women's Commission for Refugees and Children.
Available from http://www.womensrefugeecommission.org/docs/ug_ysl_toolkit.pdf

"I would much... prefer working in my field in various capacities than staying at one job that I hated for the rest of my life." — Rachelle, 23, Canada

UN Photo/Paulo Filgueiras
August 2010 | United Nations, New York

CHAPTER IV

YOUTH AT WORK

Young workers: makers and breakers

Work is central to young people's well-being. It is, of course, a requirement for income generation, but it is also a key to advancing broader social and economic development. At the individual level, a job has a direct effect on each person's self-esteem, family life as well as relations with other people. A badly paid, dangerous job at which workers' rights are not respected will have a negative effect on personal development and relationships and will fail to contribute to the development continuum.

"The key to solving problems of social exclusion and poverty is employment[...] employment is the source of social inclusion in all sorts of ways, providing not just income, but security, self realization and self esteem for workers who are organized and represented"; such is the meaning of "decent work." This statement, made by Juan Somavia, the International Labour Organization's Director-General, to the Group of Eight Labour Ministers at a Conference in 2000, is even more pertinent today than 11 years ago.[1]

Decent and productive work is thus at the centre of youth transitions into capable adulthood. The clear message from young participants on the e-discussion platform during week IV was this: job conditions for young people are difficult due to the economic crisis and, as Hasan from the Maldives said, "political chaos makes it hard for youth to be independent and live their dreams!" A lack of meaningful job opportunities (for growing youth populations) is contributing towards stagnation in the transition from youth to adulthood. For many cultures and young people, having a decent job is one significant marker towards becoming an adult.

Sadly, much of the critique of the perception of youth in Africa as "Makers and Breakers" (in a seminal book by the same name[2]) remains pertinent today. What is more, this dualistic view of young people as both innovators and destroyers is not just symptomatic in Africa (although it has particular post-colonial dimensions there), but it is widespread throughout the world. For youth, it has meant that opportunities to engage in meaningful discussion with policymakers, and to have a voice in decision-making, have been few and far between.

There are many examples of promising current work in the field of youth policy and practice on job creation and decent work, such as the work by Youth Business International (YBI), Ashoka Youth Venture, Spark, the Youth to Youth Fund and Edgeryders[3] (a European Union-funded initiative), to name a few. Furthermore, various United Nations entities, including the United Nations Human Settlements Programme (UN-HABITAT), the International Labour Organization (ILO) and the United Nations Population Fund (UNFPA) are all engaged in important work on

[1] International Labour Organization, Communication and Public Information, 2000
[2] De Boeck, Filip, and Alcinda Honwana (2005). Makers and Breakers: Children and Youth in Postcolonial Africa. London: James Currey.
[3] To read a spontaneous blog about the United Nations e-discussion from Edgeryders, see:
http://edgeryders.ppa.coe.int/blog/2011/11/young-people-talk-employment-at-un-online-forum/

youth development in general, with a major focus on employment, in close collaboration with other United Nations entities as well as youth-led organizations.

Challenges remain, however, especially real inclusivity and scale. But more than that, how we perceive new ways of working and living must be confronted collaboratively – through youth-adult partnerships and open minds. One such example on new ways of living and working was broadcast on the BBC World Service in November 2011: "The Great Reset." This programme addressed the view that opportunity, creativity and innovation arise from great economic crashes/depressions. Indeed, a comforting perspective in times of great changes.

Unemployment yes – but what about underemployment?

From 1 to 7 November 2011, week IV, the e-discussion platform was open to all to discuss their experiences at work. The e-discussion invited the views of young people aged 15 to 30,[4] as well as representatives of youth-led organizations. More than 180 comments were posted by young people from more than 76 countries across the globe. There were at least 690 people who accessed and viewed the e-discussion during the week. In addition to the e-discussion platform, there were also postings/uploads onto the United Nations International Year of Youth Facebook page, and a live question and answer Twitter session with United Nations Youth Champion, Monique Coleman, and Special Adviser to the United States Secretary of State on Global Youth Affairs, Ronan Farrow.

This chapter explores the quality and conditions of jobs held by youth, and how young people's working situation interacts with their family and home lives. While many examples were shared of young people pursuing entrepreneurial endeavours, the overall consensus was that there is a growing frustration: not only with a lack of jobs, but also a lack of engagement. The fact is that many young people need to be both listened to and collaborated with by governments and the private sector regarding job creation and workers' rights. Participants were asked, "Have you influenced any educational or employment policy forums? If so, how did you go about this and what were your successes?" The response to this question was a resounding silence. Discussion and debate with constituents on matters that affect them, such as decent work, is a constitutional obligation for many Member States which have adopted the United Nations Convention on the Rights of the Child. But more than that – it is effective policymaking.

---

[4] This takes into account both the United Nations definition of youth (15- to 24-year-olds) and many local cultural contexts and understandings.

Some of the most insightful posts on the e-discussion platform follow.

In your country, can you provide any current examples of how young people are approaching – and faring in – entrepreneurial activities?

● Several participants from Europe and Africa commented that they are currently self- employed and running their own businesses. According to Solomon in Ghana, *"lots of young graduates are starting their own companies, especially in [information and communication technologies] ICT and are making great strides."* This trend seems to be increasing among urban youth who are graduating from colleges and universities and finding it hard to secure permanent employment. Dirk from the Netherlands told us that, *"website development, as well as social businesses in Middle Eastern countries, are creating employment"* for young entrepreneurs.

● In the Dominican Republic, Maria painted a complex picture: *"Many of the private universities in the Dominican Republic offer programmes within their curricula through which students receive sponsorship to begin their business. Such new businesses fall into the categories of restaurants, entertainment, retail and technology. Since such youth are exposed to a higher level of education, they are better prepared to approach entrepreneurial activities than youth in the lower-income class."* However, she goes on to say: *"for youth in lower income classes [...] microfinance organizations have been increasing rapidly, and they facilitate the process of borrowing money to these [...] classes, allowing them to develop their business ideas. Many businesses such as small convenience stores, hair salons, drug stores and art shops have been able to develop due to the loans received from microfinance institutions."* Indeed, it is often the young men and women who have left school in order to generate extra income (to help their parents) who run most of these businesses.

ON THE UPSIDE

● Pooja from India informed us that young people in the tribal area of Chindwara are finding employment through silk production:

"Silk production is a new way for them to be employed. Tribal young farmers are earning a huge amount of money through silk production. The plan was started in villages in the year 2007 and it has changed the lives of farmers. They are getting Rs. 50,000-60,000 per acre. The Silk Department is providing free plants and financial support to tribal farmers."

- There is some degree of policy and programme support from governments: one of the examples quoted by Rachelle, 23, with Taking It Global in Canada, is the Canadian Youth Business Foundation, which *"offers young entrepreneurs aged 18-34 mentorship, learning resources and start-up financing. Since 2002, the Foundation has helped young Canadians start more than 4,000 businesses and created 18,000 jobs."*

- With regard to policy development, Hira, 22, from Pakistan highlighted the Government of Pakistan's recent development strategy, the New Growth Strategy. She informed us that:

  "This strategy talks about productivity, market reforms, creative cities, connectivity and infrastructure and youth engagement as essential pillars of a new growth model. Youth entrepreneurship is a major pillar in the framework and an implementation plan is currently being developed."

- Sergio Iriarte Quezada, week I's moderator and Knowledge Management Officer for the International Labour Organization's (ILO) Programme on Youth Employment, reminded participants this week of the ILO's Know about Business (KAB) initiative. Sergio informed us that:

  "It aims to foster positive attitudes among young people towards enterprise development and self-employment. It also creates awareness of enterprises and self-employment as a career option for young people in secondary and vocational education, and provides knowledge and information to start and operate a successful enterprise. KAB is a training programme for trainers and teachers in vocational education, secondary education and also higher education for young students between ages 15 and 18."

- According to Evona from Cameroon, *"the only way to solve the unemployment problem [...] is the creation of small and medium enterprises."*

ON THE DOWNSIDE

- Several young participants expressed concern about their government's commitment to providing opportunities for both rural and urban youth in terms of trainings, education and employment. Indeed, several young people suggested that governments should act proactively to ensure that young people are given the opportunity to be hired by private companies. Alejandro, 22, from Mexico believes that, *"[The United States and] U.S./Mexico can help by facilitating [...] youth participation [in the job market], because most of the youth are not given the right opportunities to express their skills, knowledge, talents and creative skills."*

● Participants shared the view that there are bottlenecks associated with starting one's own business. According to Solomon from Ghana, these include *"finances, office space, and tax requirements, which should be addressed proactively. If this is done, a lot more young men and women will strive to be innovative and generate incomes for themselves!"* Other challenges experienced were limited access to information, funding and support from donor agencies, international development organizations, governments and academic institutions.

● Ayshah, 26, from Kenya was keen to tell us that many young people are embracing the issue of self-employability and entrepreneurship, but:

"The major issue is lack of capital to expand their business or even start their business due to high interest rates offered by the banks here in Kenya. As far as microfinance is concerned, the intake of loans by young people is low compared to adults, [who] repay their loans more quickly than young people, despite [...] the government's [...] youth fund. [...] The terms and conditions [associated with the fund] scare us away - like collateral. Surely, where else – but from our parents – can we get [collateral]?"

Tweet Corner

Selection of some of the tweets from week IV

RT @UNpYouth: [In Ghana, lots of graduate youths r starting their own companies, especially within ICT] /Solomon http://t.co/jTufqfgG #youthjobs

RT @UNpYouth: [In Senegal, young people without higher education r more involved in entrepreneurial activities] says Amadou http://t.co/Y5IHHqhp

In your view, when it comes to gaps in decent work for young people, what are some of the major issues facing them - is it working conditions, worker rights and/or income concerns, or perhaps something else?

● The clear message from young participants was this: job conditions for young people are difficult due to the economic crisis and, as Hasan from the Maldives said, *"political chaos makes it hard for youth to be independent and live their dreams!"* One of the main concerns that Rachelle, 23, from Canada highlighted was, *"for young graduates coming out of university or college [...] the large amount of debt due to student loans. While they are eager to enter the workforce, concerns of paying off their debts may force them to take on jobs that are either outside of their field or do not pay as much as they should."* In addition, participants also pointed towards the lack of information and resources available for young people about starting up businesses/organizations, including information on business development loan schemes.

• Ayshah, 26, from Kenya raised these concerns: *"Young people work tirelessly and the pay they get for their work is little compared to those permanently employed. These days, many organizations and institutions are using internships to fill gaps that are void, thus saving resources. Very few young people are satisfied with their careers because of high competition and lack of suitable jobs in the country."*

• Maria from the Dominican Republic, believed that: *"Income concerns are what create one of the major gaps in youth employment in the Dominican Republic. Since the economic condition of the country remains unstable, young men and women worry about the salary they will receive when they start working, and mostly, will this be enough for them to sustain themselves. According to the Labour Ministry and different labour unions, the minimum wage is set in three stages, ranging between approximately US$150 to US$350, which is not enough to cover the basic needs of a household. A large number of the youth in the Dominican Republic have to use their income either to cover their expenses or to partially pay for their education. It is worthy of mention that most youth enter the job industry in the middle years of their education in order to be able to pay for it. Dominican youth are worried about being able to grow economically in the country, and also worried about how they will be able to keep up with the country's high cost of living."*

In your current job, what are the opportunities for advancement (including recognizing leadership and innovation)?

ON THE UPSIDE

• Enock, 28, from Uganda is currently working as a volunteer with the Uganda Red Cross as a peer educator. He is unpaid, but he does believe that his efforts have helped him *"learn new skills and make new friends."* He has been given on-the-job training, which is enhancing his skills and enabling him to take on more responsibilities.

• For Maria from the Dominican Republic, most of her work experiences have been in her area of interest – marketing and public relations. Although she has not secured a long-term job, she says *"internship experiences have allowed me to observe and learn about the opportunities in the market."* Currently, Maria works for the non-profit sector, conducting marketing through social media, and she believes there are many opportunities in this sector for young people.

Rachelle, 23, from Canada is working part-time as a publicist/marketing lead for a mobile advertising company and interning as a communications coordinator at a Toronto non-profit organization. According to her, she has *"learnt a lot from these two positions and [...] been given ample opportunity to take on more responsibilities. While the wages aren't the best, I am ready to take pay cuts since I don't have responsibilities such as family or mortgage, etc."* Rachelle has received on-the-job training, which has enhanced her skill set, and she tells us her *"work in both jobs has been recognized on a regular basis."*

ON THE DOWNSIDE

Erasmus, 23, from Zambia said that his current job does not provide any opportunities for advancement because it is in the informal sector. He cannot advance in his position, *"because the money I get is minimal, and with that money I can hardly save up for college education."* He went on to say that, *"the management in the office does not listen to my ideas because of my lesser experience and qualifications as compared to the permanent staff in the office."*

Share with us your personal experiences of working in the informal economy. What have been the benefits and the challenges?

Precious, 26, from Nigeria said that although she does not have personal experience working in the informal sector, she does work with youth both in school and out of school who do have such experience. *"Some youth are doing well, depending on their location and the amount of resources invested in the business they are working in. While for others the benefits they acquire are helping them build their own skills."*

Precious went on to say: *"Some of the challenges they are facing include: 1) For one domestic worker, lack of trust by the owner (of the place), which hinders a proper relationship; 2) Lack of funds to equip the informal [business], thereby making the work hectic and cumbersome; 3) Over-use [exploitation] of youth working in this area, because there are few benefits; 4) For street vendors, one of the major challenges is the [...risk of falling] sick, because of the working environment [and the lack of safeguards]."*

Lody, 25, from Cambodia reminded us of the gender inequalities that persist, commenting that: *"Young women are doubly affected as they face not only lack of opportunities, but poor quality of work, especially in the informal [sector] – characterized by low wages, less secure employment, and [often limited] representation."*

Vote Corner

If you were the Chief Executive of a large foundation, where would you spend your money in order to increase and improve youth employment, both within and beyond your organization?

The top three recommendations selected from the e-discussion platform and voted on by participants on the International Year of the Youth Facebook page were:

1) Open up vocational training institutes for both rural and urban youth (64 per cent of votes)
2) Focus on empowering youth through small grants (19 per cent of votes)
3) Sponsor secondary education for marginalized young people (17 per cent of votes)

WHAT YOUNG PEOPLE SAY

- Shruti, 24, from Mumbai, India, said that if she was a Chief Executive, she would invest within her organization *"in building youth ambassadors [...] who have been-there-done-that and can prove a good role model for the students/youth outside my organization. [Each of] these youth ambassadors would be responsible for mentoring at least one underprivileged young person."*

- Karuna, 23, also from India said that she would create a paid internship programme for fresh graduates within her organization. *"Paid internships can help with both a decent income and experience. Outside the organization, I would promote corporate social responsibility strategies and create capacity-building and skills development courses and workshops for young people."*

Several of the other recommendations included:

- Invest in social businesses led by and focused on employing young people

- Invest money in improving community relations and employment opportunities for young graduates

- Provide field-specific scholarships for college and university students

- Invest in a strong internship programme that would recruit new graduates to work for my company for an extended period of time; for example, the Ontario government has a highly selective and popular two-year internship programme, after which young people get to work with Ontario ministries (Canada)

- Create a pool of funds to invest in young entrepreneurs

- Align scholarship opportunities to communities; decentralize opportunities to universities or private businesses and allow them to select the candidates

- Invest in information and communication technologies and provide leadership opportunities to young people through trainings in the private and non-profit sectors

How have your job and working conditions affected your family life and well-being? Including your relationships with parents and siblings and/or your own children and spouse; age of marriage and starting a family; living arrangements; etc.?

- Karuna, 23, from India focused on her relationship with her parents, telling us, *"it has changed"* since she finished her studies and started working. *"It's now awkward to ask for money from my parents. While I am earning, some of my friends are not, and they are graduates. They face the same problem with their parents and minor discussions on money do crop up."* According to Karuna, joblessness implies *"a lack of financial resources - which implies stress. And speaking of health, my job has provided me with a good health insurance package that has helped me a great deal! I feel more secure about my health."*

- Rachelle, 23, from Toronto, Canada said that her work has *"not really impacted"* her family life. Yet, for the most part, her work means that she *"is rarely home and, at times when I am at home, I am doing work."* Ideally, she would prefer not to take her work home. She feels lucky to be living with her parents since she is not paying any rent, and because of this she has been able to save money to further her education. Prior to her current two part-time jobs, she was working full-time in a work environment that she found stressful and did not like. *"I would much [...] prefer working in my field in various capacities than staying at one job that I hated for the rest of my life."*

How are you promoting and raising awareness about green jobs?

- Enass, 25, from Jordan emphasized that the profile and potential of green jobs needs to be raised:

  "We can ensure that graduates and other job seekers will be looking for environmental sustainability courses and trainings in order to be able to meet new job demands. At the same time, training centres and other educational institutions will provide this instruction and, as a result, this will increase the awareness about green jobs."

- Several participants also recalled the importance of advocacy, such as creating online blogs to discuss and highlight development issues related to the June 2012 United Nations Conference on Sustainable Development, Rio+20. In addition, in October 2011, the United Nations Environmental Programme (UNEP) held a workshop to showcase the green projects of young environmental leaders from 18 developing countries, thus contributing towards raising the profile of young activists.

- Michael, 23, from Italy commented that, *"in relation to Rio+20, the World Esperanto Youth Organization co-authored a document to help guide the compilation of the zero-draft of the final outcome document, as [the Organization is] convinced that social equity is a key part of sustainable development."*

- Dirk, Youth Delegate of the Netherlands to the United Nations, shared: *"I am part of the global youth movement that is trying to push the Dutch ministry and opinion leaders towards progressive, ambitious, just and socially sustainable goals at the Rio+20 summit. Let's see what this youth movement can achieve!"*

- Esther also informed us on the Facebook page of the 6th annual African Economic Conference on the theme, Green Economy and Structural Transformation. Esther posted that *"African youth call for the development of green job opportunities within the African green economy agenda and the promotion of African youth entrepreneurship. Youths insist that the jobs created remain with indigenous African youth."*

- Sarah, 24, from Kenya provided some examples, commenting that she has been involved in the Youth Agency for Development of Science, Technology & Innovation (YADSTI) and Rotaract, whereby she is giving back to her community through tree planting. *"At a time when the Mau forest [...] was almost destroyed due to massive deforestation, under YADSTI we went to the forest and planted more than eleven hectares of trees!"* There are several green entrepreneurial activities in Kenya at present, including by the Youth Entrepreneurship Facility, a partnership among the Africa Commission, the Youth Employment Network and the International Labour Organization.

● Participants also discussed other activities that bring in income through green jobs, such as mushroom farming, bee keeping and fruit harvesting. For example, there is an emerging market in Nepal's farming sector for medicinal herbs and trees.

Are you involved in any philanthropic work?

The posts received on the e-discussion platform focused on personal stories of philanthropy. They included:

● Kayode from Nigeria, who leads a team of young people between the ages of 18 and 35 at the organization, Joint Initiative for Development, expressed concern that:

"Nigeria's unemployment figure stands at 21 per cent, with youths forming the largest percentage. Nigeria stands to benefit from a huge number of young [people in the] workforce in the next 30 years if, and only if, these youths are engaged effectively and given opportunities. Currently, the number of graduates turned out from our institution is growing [in] negative proportion to the number of available jobs. The private sector is unsatisfied with the quality of graduates."

● Nanteza, 26, from Uganda is with the National Youth Empowerment Network. She works with young people to help them *"sustain themselves and [emerge from] poverty."* Among the various undertakings of the network are the Wagari Girls project, Kakunyu brick making project, a nursery and primary school and a football academy. Nanteza told us:

"The Wagari Girls project was started to empower the girl child [through developing] various skills such as making tablecloths, mats, beads, cards, polythene bags, baskets, necklaces and bangles. And the Kakunyu brick making project was started to help the young men and boys in this village. This project has taught the boys various skills such as making bricks, tiles and ventilators out of clay. The project involved 15 boys, [who] sold 20,000 bricks [...] One of the young boys of this project, Richard [...] has started making his own bricks and he is in the final stages of the process."

● Amadou, 24, from Senegal shared that he has co-created – with a group of students – an association called "Action-Etudiant pour la petite enfance" (Student Action for Early Childhood). The main objective of this association is to support a rural nursery school near the university. Amadou collects money to buy notebooks, books and pencils for the children. He also organizes entertainment activities for the children such as the annual "Holiday for Hope," and, in 2010, he organized a medical visit for rural children who lacked medical care. Through collaboration with the university hospital, these children are now being treated at no cost.

Twitterview with

United Nations Youth Champion, Monique Coleman,
and Special Advisor on Global Youth Issues to
the United States Secretary of State, Ronan Farrow

United Nations Youth Champion, Monique Coleman (@gimmemotalk), and Special Advisor on Global Youth Issues to the United States Secretary of State, Ronan Farrow (@RonanFarrow), were hosted by the United Nations Focal Point on Youth for a one-hour Twitter interview on: twitter.com/UNpYouth. Youth from around the world posed questions to the special guests about various aspects of youth employment. Monique and Ronan both encouraged decision-makers to "do more" and "partner with youth!" Some of the notable quotes from Ronan and Monique included:

Ronan Farrow on disability
@amdia More countries must adopt legislation protecting disabled. @StateDept has office on this issue. Check @Disabilitygov too. #youthjobs — @RonanFarrow

@amdia Grew up w/ disabled siblings & disabled joblessness is key concern for me. It should be for world too; untapped workforce. #youthjobs — @RonanFarrow

On strengthening the youth agendas of donors
@nicolashepherd Need strong message from key donors to partner w/ youth, respond to youth populations. Current action not enough. #youthjobs — @RonanFarrow

On youth engagement
Great to hear twittocracy out on #youthjobs. More work needs to be done – but clearly we have tremendous energy in this community to do it. — @RonanFarrow

Monique Coleman on livelihoods
@gimmemotalk what are the baby steps to recognize our own value and potential? #youthjobs — @sanrarefira

@sanrarefira 1st discover your passions! Your true interests always lead to a positive outcome #youthjobs — @gimmemotalk

@sanrarefira 2nd figure out what you're good at & work to get even better #youthjobs — @gimmemotalk

@sanrarefira Lastly, marry the two. See how your passions and skills can be applied toward social change #youthjobs — @gimmemotalk

Some of the notable comments sent to Monique and Ronan by young people included:

@gimmemotalk I totally agree. we have to 'demonstrate' and not 'talk' that investing in girls pays #youthjobs — @ESTHERCLIMATE

@Karanja_Anthony @gimmemotalk many economists & philosophers agree that work is one way we naturally express our inherent value. —@ LEROYLAMAR

@UNpYouth @gimmemotalk @ronanfarrow @GirlUp low self esteem of the youth undermines their potential mentorship can help overcome #youthjobs —@NICOLEMWAYNE

@rajneeshb MDGs will adress the illiteracy part, but we need to factor individual gov't participation in ensuring quality edu #youthjobs — @ KARANJA_ANTHONY

We as #youth have opp to effect positive #change... so let's shake up status quo. I think the world will listen! Eh @RonanFarrow? #youthjobs — @ ERINSCHRODE

CHAPTER CONCLUSIONS

Despite the global financial turmoil, and the huge concerns many young people have regarding their future job opportunities, many youth out there are makers – not breakers. This is evident on many social networking sites, such as Youth Partnership, One Young World Chad and Africa Youth Day 2011. While it is difficult to ascertain the level of impact, there is hope.

According to the majority of participants on the e-discussion platform, there is a growing swell of young entrepreneurs starting small businesses; some out of choice and others out of necessity. Maria from the Dominican Republic reminded us that youth *"exposed to a higher level of education [...] are [more likely to be] better prepared to approach entrepreneurial activities than youth in the lower-income class."*

One such young entrepreneur is Awa from Cameroon, who shared with us his vision:

"I created a social enterprise in 2009, Impact Creators, and I have been delivering trainings on personal development in different institutes of higher learning. One of the recent programmes we want to implement is called Career Orientation and Development + Skills (CODES). The general objective of the programme is to train (coach) the students and young professionals on personal and professional development. Using the career development cycle, we have identified different training topics that will be developed and delivered, as we contribute to bridging the gap between school and the world of work. Impact Creator's SHINE (Share Information Network) platform will then serve as an interface between the beneficiaries and career-related scholarships, fellowships and job opportunities, inter alia, at the national and international levels."

Having said this, times are very tough: participants expressed concerns over job insecurity, lack of engagement with policymakers, rising living and business costs, and paying off student debts – to name but a few. The clear message from young participants was this: job conditions for young people are difficult due to the economic crisis and, as Hasan from the Maldives said, *"political chaos makes it hard for youth to be independent and live their dreams!"*

Indeed, Juan Somavia, the International Labour Organization's Director-General, reminded us at the beginning of this chapter: employment is the source of social inclusion in all sorts of ways, providing not just income, but security, self-realization and self- esteem. This decent work agenda has all sorts of wider implications for society. Its antithesis – a lack of meaningful job opportunities – is potentially very destructive; at both a personal and a societal level. Hence, a lack of decent jobs is currently contributing towards stagnation in the transition for young people from youth to adulthood. Having a decent job is one significant milestone towards enabling a young person to become an adult change agent and an active citizen in their community.

@netalejandro reminds us of the potential of young philanthropists and entrepreneurs, and leaves us with this thought:

"Just as business entrepreneurs create and transform whole industries, social entrepreneurs act as the change agents for society, seizing opportunities others miss in order to improve systems, invent and disseminate new approaches and advance sustainable solutions that create social value in different kinds of services or products."

CASE STUDY
Hira, 23-year-old woman from Pakistan

pending my adolescent years in rural Balochistan, and my adulthood in urban Lahore, opened my eyes to new insights about attitudes and living styles of my people.

My father, a civil servant, was required to move around different areas of Pakistan as part of his job, which led to frequent changes of educational institutes at a young age, which was difficult for me to get accustomed to. This shifting between locations did, however, allow me to observe cultural differences between urban and rural places in my country. These differences were sometimes quite significant; in Balochistan, women would hide themselves at the slightest breach of privacy, whereas in Lahore, they would confidently fight to gain the space to be heard.

This experience exposed me to problems that were common in the transition from adolescence to youth, which was often associated with emotional stress. For example, I was unable to focus on my studies due to the frequent change of learning environments. As a 9th grader, my anxiety found a vent in an internship at a local hospital in Lahore, where I met women and children deprived of their basic needs. Deeply grieved, and although I could do little to change their situation, I felt overwhelmingly thankful for being born in a more progressive family, where women are allowed to study and work.

Nevertheless, six months later, I started volunteering in development work for children in Pakistan, which eventually opened a great opportunity for me to intern with an international development organization in New York. There, I became inspired by the potential of leadership. When I returned home, I continued to volunteer with a youth programme there in addition to working in my first paying job. This made me feel empowered and trusted by my colleagues at the programme, as I introduced activities and projects for young people. Through this voluntary work, I realized that empowerment is necessary for young Pakistani women and men to progress in life.

I travelled the world and met similar young people who were doing greater things and making a greater impact. This inspired me, at the age of 21, to co-found a non- governmental organization (NGO) called Youth Dividend. The NGO was created with the idea to embrace youth empowerment and participation in formulating policies that define their future.

Establishing Youth Dividend and getting it running was not easy. I was introduced to hundreds of hurdles in registering the NGO, so the processes took a long time. No work could be done without sitting for ridiculously long hours in registration offices, and having to establish contacts with big bosses. Added to this were issues around the induction of volunteers, who did not agree to work without monetary compensation, as well as challenges related to mobilizing funding and managing operations while also working full time.

During the first few months, I ran the organization's operations through savings I had made from my salary. I connected with NGO partners through online blogs, and created a pool of advisors for the NGO through networking while participating in conferences.

All of these experiences taught me that nothing in life comes easy - where there is passion, there is struggle, and where there is struggle, there are great results!

After more than 4 years working in the development field, I am now pursuing a graduate degree at Cornell University. I felt the need to attain higher education to access good academic mentoring and to expand my horizons, and eventually to make a difference in the lives of people at the policy level.

Additional resources

International Labour Organization (2007). Toolkit for mainstreaming employment and decent work. Geneva: International Labour Organization. Available from http://www.ilo.org/public/english/bureau/pardev/download/toolkit_en.pdf

Network for Youth in Transitions: current resources on youth and livelihoods. For more information http://networkforyouthintransition.org/forum/categories/youth-and- livelihood/listForCategory

Road to Rio plus 20: global youth mobilization initiative working towards the United Nations Conference on Sustainable Development in Brazil in June 2012, Rio+20. For more information www.roadtorioplus20.org

The 5th Global YES Summit (Rework the World): focus on youth entrepreneurship. For more information http://www.reworktheworld.org/Projects/tabid/595/Default.aspx

Van der Geest, Kees (2010). Rural youth employment in developing countries: a global view. Rural Employment - Overview/Synthesis, #1 (March). Rome: Food and Agriculture Organization of the United Nations. Available from http://www.fao-ilo.org/fileadmin/user_upload /fao_ilo/pdf/V andergeest_2010_RurY outhEmpl_150_ppi.pdf

Youth Business International (2011). Youth entrepreneurship: closing the gap.
London: Youth Business International. Available from http://www.youthbusiness.org/pdf/YBI%20Closing%20The%20Gap.pdf

YouthSave Consortium: sharing lessons and resources on delivering youth savings services. For more information http://youthsave.org/content/youthsave-project-launches- new-website

CONCLUSIONS AND RECOMMENDATIONS

"Paid internships can help with both a decent income and experience. Outside the organization, I would promote corporate social responsibility strategies and create capacity-building and skills development courses and workshops for young people."
–Karuna, 23, India

UN Photo/Paulo Filgueiras
Monique Coleman (left), UN Champion for Youth
November 2011 | United Nations, New York

Conclusions

The United Nations e-discussion on youth employment held from 11 October to 7 November received approximately 1,100 comments from young people around the world. Their contributions addressed various aspects of overcoming challenges to finding decent work, better aligning educational systems and skills development with labour market needs, as well as the social implications of employment trends on the lives of young people.

Many young people shared common key employment concerns. Participants questioned the quality of education they and their peers receive: whether or not it is relevant to available jobs, how their knowledge and skills will serve them in the long-term, and the extent to which decision-makers are committed to needed investment in the potential of young people. They are frustrated by high rates of unemployment, which is causing many youth to rely on volunteerism in order to gain experience, and even affecting students who are unable to find part-time work to help support their studies. Young women in particular confront barriers to employment, including job segregation and salary discrimination. When young people do obtain jobs, they often involve poor wages as well as working conditions, including long hours, insecurity and a lack of health and other benefits, which do not allow them to be independent and provide for family. Moreover, although some young people shared positive views of accessing job opportunities through migration, many reported growing concern that in order to secure even low-level jobs, they would have to leave their homes and families.

Throughout the progression of the four-week e-discussion, young people's comments reflected the full spectrum of negative and positive outlooks. They exhibited considerable energy and enthusiasm not only by focusing on obstacles to full and decent employment, but also by using the platform as a motivational space to encourage others and share good practices and success stories on how to go about securing productive and decent work. Although some participants expressed little or no optimism regarding the state of youth employment, several seemed to succeed in inspiring hope in others.

Chapter II revealed that young people view many higher educational systems and institutions as inadequately tailored to the actual dynamic needs of the labour market. They reported that formal education curricula are often overly theoretical, leaving students feeling ill-prepared and lacking the necessary practical skills for the labour force. Some students consequently delay their entry into the job market to continue their studies or seek out low-level jobs. More and better linkages are therefore needed between learning institutions and employers. Young people further pointed out a gap in quality between private and public educational institutions that provides graduates of private schools with a competitive advantage in the labour market.

Young people shared more positive views of non-formal education, which they believe can both complement formal education with important distinct skills and also serve as an important resource for youth without access to formal education. Participants further attached value to vocational education as a means for job preparedness, though found inadequate opportunities to access it and expressed concern about how likely it is to lead to decent work. On the whole, young people additionally felt that internships and volunteerism offer opportunities to develop life skills and improve employment prospects, including in entrepreneurship.

Chapter II highlighted two key messages for young people's job preparedness. The first was that leadership qualities must be developed among youth not only to foster empowerment, but also to fuel innovative solutions to youth employment challenges. The second was the need to encourage young people to be proactive in pursuing their livelihood aspirations.

Chapter III revealed that young people are finding and making use of a range of tools, where available, to help them find jobs, with formal and informal business and social network proving to be the most valuable sources of career information and guidance. The majority of participants were either unemployed, still completing their educational programmes, performing unpaid or part-time work, working on short-term contracts or in "small jobs," or engaged in several of these activities. Amidst widespread unemployment and in order to gain work experience, some are either engaged in internship programmes or volunteer positions. A point that emerged strongly from the e- discussion was that young people prefer to be active rather than to "sit around"; they bear the conditions of underemployment in the belief that their perseverance, experience and enthusiasm will be rewarded in the future.

Participants identified emerging opportunities for youth employment in new types of jobs in the fields of information and communication technologies (ITCs), social networking and environmental sustainability ("green jobs"). Many young people reported that their ideal job is to work in – or to create – green jobs for the future. There was no clear consensus as to whether globalization (as represented by such factors as use of ICTs or working abroad, etc.) is, in general, favourable or not, as participants recognized both advantages and disadvantages. However, there was broad agreement that self-motivation, dedication, patience and a positive outlook are key elements of successful job searching.

Chapter IV underscored that a decent job is a marker of adulthood, independence and active citizenship. Yet the lack of decent jobs today is hindering this period of transition for young people and their future economic participation. Young people shared their concerns about gaps in access to decent work, particularly amidst the economic crisis. Participants expressed worries related to job insecurity, citing the prevalence of short-term contracts; low wages, amidst rising costs of living; difficulties in obtaining adequate practical work experience, with some youth calling for such requirements in educational institutions; few opportunities for workplace advancement; debts, including student loans; and family well-being.

Young people identified the creation of small- and medium-sized enterprises as an important and effective means to overcome high unemployment rates and poor working conditions. In fact, the majority of participants noted a growing number of young entrepreneurs starting their own businesses – some out of choice and others due to a lack of other employment options – with many examples of success and promise, including in social entrepreneurship. However, young people also noted that practical information and guidance on entrepreneurial initiatives as well as financing opportunities are often difficult for them to access.

Chapter IV asserted that, despite the current youth employment challenge, most young people are makers rather than breakers. Although many youth conveyed a lack of confidence in their futures, there remains – nonetheless – hope.

Societies cannot afford to neglect young people and their skills, knowledge, energy and potential. They cannot expect young people to study hard and word hard as the traditional means to decent work and success, amidst diminishing evidence of its effectiveness. Young people require financial and social investments to fulfil their potential, to transition into adulthood and to be active and engaged citizens. Decent jobs not only contribute to young people's lifetime employment success, they have a proven multiplier effect on family well-being, the health of national economies and societies at large.

We thank Navjot K. for sharing these concluding words on behalf of youth: *"We want to make a difference. We want a chance to work. We want to prove ourselves."*

Recommendations[1]

Based on the conclusions the main recommendations are...

CHAPTER II'S VOTE CORNER:
What are your top 1-3 recommendations for policymakers towards ensuring young people are adequately and appropriately prepared for the job market?

The top three recommendations as voted by participants on the International Year of the Youth Facebook page were:

[1] These are reproduced from each week's/chapter's vote corner.

1) Provide practical opportunities and encourage entrepreneurship and alternative careers (72 per cent of votes);

2) After policies are put in place, ensure that they are enforced and implemented (17 per cent of votes);

3) Ensure practices in the work place are inclusive, non-discriminatory and promote equal opportunities (11 per cent of votes).

In addition to the above, several other recommendations were proposed. Most notably:

- The majority agreed there is a need to improve the quality of education and to make it accessible to all young people. This requires tailoring curricula more effectively to the labour market, including through the development of practical skills (proposed by Muhamad, 20, with the Asian Law Students Association).

- Mechanisms should be put in place by governments in partnership with the private sector; so that institutions are supporting internships and vocational training at scale and in a broad range of disciplines.

- Vocational training, apprenticeships and non-formal education should be more widely recognized by employers as valuable components of a rounded education, which in turn would increase candidates' employment credentials and contribute towards a more stable labour market.

- All governments should provide spaces for young people to share their views and discuss the issues they face with regard to education and employment (Yasmyn, 24, from Guadeloupe).

- Governments and the private sector should ensure that information is widely available to all segments of the youth population and support those social groups which experience the most difficulties in accessing and completing education, such as young people living in extreme poverty and in rural locations, young women and youth with disabilities.

- Yanira, 29, from Mexico suggested the following:

"1) I recommend that before graduating from university, the government should assist with internship programmes at prestigious companies, whereby youth can acquire responsibilities and increase their competitive qualities. 2) According to the labour market, the government should create a fund to train young leaders in all of the main national educational institutions. They would promote the scheme internationally as well. 3) Design a strategy between governments and students, in which young people demonstrate their capabilities through community service, applying their knowledge in other countries, and empowering them to develop their team skills – preparing them for a working life."

CHAPTER III'S VOTE CORNER
What are your top three tips for other young job hunters?

After several suggestions were submitted to the e-discussion platform, participants voted on the most talked-about submissions via the Facebook page. The top three tips were:

1) Ambition: have a "can do" attitude, take action and make things happen. This tip received 66 per cent of the votes.

   This can be done through working on the way one presents oneself, or by using volunteering as a way to a more stable job or to starting one's own business. Sibeso, a 25- year-old female from Zambia working with the United Nations Youth Association of Zambia (YUNA ZAMBIA), wrote: *"My fellow youths, I would advise you to start becoming your own bosses by starting up your own businesses, rather than waiting to get employed. Remember: we are not growing any younger–but older –by the day."*

2) Perseverance: do not give up. This received 18 per cent of the votes.

   Tinghua stated: *"Always look on the bright side of life: If you failed a job interview, at least you accumulated interview experience."*

3) Social networks (formal or informal) – build and make use of these. This also received 18 per cent of the votes.

   Joe, 24, from the United Kingdom, who has never been unemployed, explained how he had spent months working to help his friends find jobs: by improving their CVs, giving interview advice and organizing interviews. Four of his friends have now secured jobs. He stated: *"Your friends with jobs have knowledge about the process. Get that knowledge. If you have a job, share your knowledge with others."*

CHAPTER IV'S VOTE CORNER
If you were the Chief Executive of a large foundation, where would you spend your money in order to increase and improve youth employment, both within and beyond your organization?

● Shruti, 24, from Mumbai, India, said that if she was a Chief Executive, she would invest within her organization *"in building youth ambassadors [...] who have been- there-done-that and can prove a good role model for the students/youth outside my organization. [Each of] these youth ambassadors would be responsible for mentoring at least one underprivileged young person."*

Karuna, 23, also from India said that she would create a paid internship programme for fresh graduates within her organization. *"Paid internships can help with both a decent income and experience. Outside the organization, I would promote corporate social responsibility strategies and create capacity-building and skills development courses and workshops for young people."*

The top three recommendations selected from the e-discussion platform and voted on by participants on the International Year of the Youth Facebook page were:

1) Open up vocational training institutes for both rural and urban youth (64 per cent of votes)
2) Focus on empowering youth through small grants (19 per cent of votes)
3) Sponsor secondary education for marginalized young people (17 per cent of votes)

Several of the other recommendations included:

● Invest in social businesses led by and focused on employing young people

● Invest money in improving community relations and employment opportunities for young graduates

● Provide field-specific scholarships for college and university students

● Invest in a strong internship programme that would recruit new graduates to work for my company for an extended period of time; for example, the Ontario [provincial] government has a highly selective and popular two-year internship programme, after which young people get to work with Ontario Ministries (Canada)

● Create a pool of funds to invest in young entrepreneurs

● Align scholarship opportunities to communities; decentralize opportunities to universities or private businesses and allow them to select the candidates

● Invest in information and communication technologies and provide leadership opportunities to young people through trainings in the private and non-profit sectors

Resources

Information on youth participation in creating national action plans from "Review of national action plans on youth employment: putting commitment into action" (United Nations, Department of Economic and Social Affairs, 2007):

"In some countries efforts are underway to create 'a space at the table' for youth participation in the decision-making processes through formal mechanisms such as youth advisory groups or the creation of a youth 'seat' in national coordinating structures designing and implementing [national action plans] NAPs. It is evident that some governments are meeting their commitment to involve youth in the development of National Action Plans, but significantly more effort must be made not only to promote youth employment as a central development issue for Member States, but also to ensure the active involvement of youth and youth organizations in policy development at all levels" (p. 23).

For a country case study on the Democratic Republic of Congo (DRC) (Youth Employment Network): http://www.ilo.org/public/english/employment/yen/whatwedo/success/alice.htm

"[The Youth Employment Network] YEN-DRC and YWCA continued to lobby the government for accession to the YEN. On May 22, 2005, our cries were finally heard when the President signed a letter to the UN Secretary-General requesting our country to become a YEN Lead Country.

Since that time I have been heavily involved in the drafting of DRC's [National Action Plan] NAP on Youth Employment including the coordination of the Youth Consultative Group. The Youth Consultative Group is responsible for youth inputs on the NAP development process alongside the government, [the United Nations Development Programme] UNDP and [the International Labour Organization] ILO."

Youth Employment Inventory (YEI) - information on youth employment interventions around the world: http://www.youth-employment-inventory.org

References

Allen, Katie (2011). Youth Unemployment Hits 1 Million. The Guardian, 16 November, Business.

British Broadcasting Corporation (2011). World Biz Podcast: The Great Reset. Accessed 6 November 2011.

Chamie, Joseph (2011). A 'Youth Bulge' Feeds Arab Discontent. The Daily Star, 15 April, Commentary, p. 7.

De Boeck, Filip, and Alcinda Honwana (2005). Makers and Breakers: Children and Youth in Postcolonial Africa. London: James Currey.

European Commission (2011). Eurostat Unemployment Statistics, data up to October 2011. Available from http://epp.eurostat.ec.europa.eu/statistics_explained/index.php/Unemployment_statistics

International Labour Organization (2010). Global Employment Trends for Youth: Special issue on the impact of the global economic crisis on youth. Geneva: International Labour Office.

International Labour Organization (2011a). Global Employment Trends 2011: the challenge of a jobs recovery. Geneva: International Labour Office.

International Labour Organization (2011b). Global Employment Trends for Youth: 2011 update. Geneva: International Labour Office.

International Labour Organization, Communication and Public Information (2000). Press release: ILO Director-General highlights need for 'Decent Work', 10 November 2000, ILO/00/42. Available from http://www.ilo.org/global/about-the-ilo/press-and-mediacentre/news/WCMS_007916/lang--en/index.htm

International Labour Organization, International Institute for Labour Studies (2010). World of Work Report 2010: From one crisis to the next? Geneva: International Labour Office.

International Labour Organization, International Programme on the Elimination of Child Labour (2011). Children in Hazardous Work: What we know, what we need to do. Geneva: International Labour Office.

International Labour Organization, Regional Office for Latin America and the Caribbean (2009). Panorama Laboral 2009. Lima: International Labour Organization, Regional Office for Latin America and the Caribbean, p. 52.

Kahn, Lauren, Mary Abdo, Sarah Hewes and others (2011). The Way to Work: young people speak out on transitions to employment. The Youth of Today. Available from: http://www.youngfoundation.org/files/images/The_Way_to_Work.pdf.

Kim, Soo-yeon (2011). Economic burdens prompting Koreans to delay marriage. Yonhap News, 10 January.

Organization for Economic Cooperation and Development (2011). OECD Employment Outlook 2011. Organization for Economic Cooperation and Development.

Rocyn-Jones, Gemma (2011). Youth unemployment: looking past the headlines. Blog for the Young Foundation. Available from http://www.youngfoundation.org/blog/youth-leadership/youth-unemployment-looking-past-headlines. Accessed 6 November 2011.

Secretariat of the Africa Commission (2009). Realizing the Potential of Africa's Youth. Copenhagen: Ministry of Foreign Affairs of Denmark. Available from http://www.africacommission.um.dk/NR/rdonlyres/3B1B9EC7-98C9-4EB1-84F0-1132B5DCFBBF/0/ReportoftheAfricaCommission2ndedition.pdf

South African Institute of Race Relations (2011). One in Two Youths Unemployed. Press Release 31 January 2011. Unpublished. Available from http://www.sairr.org.za/media/mediareleases/One%20in%20two%20youths%20unemployed%20-%2031%20January%202011.pdf/view?searchterm=youth+unem

Stobbe, Mike (2011). Lower Birth Rates for Young Women Tied to Economy. Associated Press, 17 November.

United Nations (1995). World Programme of Action for Youth to the Year 2000 and Beyond. General Assembly resolution 50/81 of 14 December 1995. A/RES/50/81. Available from http://www.un.org/Docs/journal/asp/ws.asp?m=A/RES/50/81

United Nations, Department of Economic and Social Affairs (2007). Review of National Action Plans on Youth Employment: putting commitment into action. New York: United Nations. Available from http://www.un.org/esa/socdev/publications/National-Action- Plans.pdf.

United Nations, Department of Economic and Social Affairs, Population Division (2011). World Population Prospects, the 2010 Revision. New York: United Nations.

United Nations, Department of Public Information (2011). Empowering youth is key to lasting peace, sustainable development, stresses Deputy Secretary-General in address at African Union Summit. Press release, DSG/SM/564, AFR/2204, 1 July. Available from http://www.un.org/News/Press/docs/2011/dsgsm564.doc.htm

United Nations, Economic Commission for Africa (2011). Africa Youth Report 2011: Addressing the youth education and employment nexus in the new global economy. Addis Ababa: United Nations Economic Commission for Africa. Available from http://www.uneca.org/ayr2011/African%20Youth%20Report_2011_Final.pdf

United Nations, Educational, Scientific and Cultural Organization (2011a). The Education for All Global Monitoring Report 2011: The hidden crisis - armed conflict and education. Paris: United Nations Educational, Scientific and Cultural Organization. Available from http://www.unesco.org/new/en/education/themes/leading-the-international-agenda/efareport/reports/2011-conflict/

United Nations, Educational, Scientific and Cultural Organization (2011b). Final report of the 7th UNESCO Youth Forum. 26 October. 36 C/47. Available from http://unesdoc.unesco.org/images/0021/002134/213427e.pdf

United Nations, Educational, Scientific and Cultural Organization (1997). International Standard Classification of Education - ISCED 1997. November.

United Nations, Human Settlements Programme (2010). State of the Urban Youth 2010/2011: Leveling the playing field. London: Earthscan. Available from http://www.unhabitat.org/pmss/listItemDetails.aspx?publicationID=2928

World Bank (2010). "Ready for work? Increasing Economic Opportunity for Adolescent Girls and Young Women." Washington, D.C.: World Bank. Available from http://siteresources.worldbank.org/EXTGENDER/Resources/AGI-Ready-to- W ork_2010.pdf

X Central European Initiative (2010). Draft report of the X CEI Youth Forum on education and employment of young people – challenges and perspectives, organized by the Directorate of Youth and Sport of Montenegro, with financial support from the Central European Initiative Secretariat, Budva, Montenegro, 25 and 26 November 2010. Available from http://www.infomladi.me/fajlovi/mladi/attach_fajlovi/eng/news/ youth- office/2010/12/pdf/draft_report_x_cei_youth_forum.pdf

Youth Employment Network. Youth play a vital role in DRC's (Democratic Republic of the Congo) accession as a YEN Lead Country and the NAP development. Available from http://www.ilo.org/public/english/employment/yen/whatwedo/success/alice.htm

UNWorldYouthReport.org

Published by the United Nations Department of Economic and Social Affairs